A Guide in the Study of the Usage of the American English

A Compilation of Some Rules of Grammar as Applied and Explained

Ernesto L. Lasafin

Ukiyoto Publishing

All global publishing rights are held by

Ukiyoto Publishing

Published in 2024

Content Copyright © Ernesto L. Lasafin

ISBN 9789367958377

All rights reserved.

No part of this publication may be reproduced, transmitted, or stored in a retrieval system, in any form by any means, electronic, mechanical, photocopying, recording or otherwise, without the prior permission of the publisher.

The moral rights of the author have been asserted.

This book is sold subject to the condition that it shall not by way of trade or otherwise, be lent, resold, hired out or otherwise circulated, without the publisher's prior consent, in any form of binding or cover other than that in which it is published.

www.ukiyoto.com

Thank you, my friend, W. J. Manares, who helped me in the publishing of this useful book. Thanks to Ukiyoto House, Philippines for the assistance. Thank you, my family, my friends, and my colleagues, who supports me by all means.

Contents

Preface	1
A Guide To The Study Of The English Grammar	3
The English Sentence Structure And Its Two Main Parts	36
Some Common Expressions In English Usage	165
About the Author	*208*

Preface

The discouraging decline of the quality of education in the Philippines today is a serious concern for all of us Filipinos. Everyone must do his share in addressing the problem of the low quality of Philippine education, which is a contributory factor to the slow growth of the national economy.

The Philippine educational system failed to sustain the fluency in the use of English as a medium of interaction that pre-World War II Filipinos enjoyed. Then, almost all graduates of the elementary grades spoke good English, the universal language. Now, many teachers do not have a good grasp or working knowledge of English as a medium of instruction in the public schools. In general, students are hesitant to speak in English for many reasons.

It is believed that as the students gain a working knowledge of the English structural grammar, using the English language that can be understood by English-speaking natives will be easy. A late pre-World War II teacher said then that one of the causes of the failure of students to communicate in English is their having not learned the basic English grammar. As a result, students are reluctant to speak in English, lest others laugh at them for their stuttering English utterances.

The mastery of the basic mechanics of modern English will encourage the students to use good English in oral and written communication. It is hoped that the students would be effectively aided in learning the basic mechanics of good English grammar through the use of these guide notes. Phrases and clauses are used in the explanation in these guide notes to make it easy for the students to understand.

Some students may find these notes repetitive, but repetition will help the slow learners. Based on the modern approach to the study of English structural grammar, these guide notes were compiled, edited and used as supplementary teaching materials in teaching the English grammar to secondary school students of a national school in Iloilo.

2   A Guide in the Study of the Usage of the American English

Any correction to the errors the readers might find in this compilation is very much welcome.

ERNESTO L. LASAFIN, M.A. Ed.

A Guide To The Study Of The English Grammar

Communication in the English Language

All creatures of God on earth need to communicate with one another. Among human beings, communication is made by means of utterance or written words. The organized system of speech is language. Words are the basic units of language. When one speaks or writes, he puts words together in a sentence. Thus, language is not just words; it is <u>words</u> strung together in coherent sentences to be used for communication.

English is the universal medium of communication. People who can communicate effectively in the English language are the ones likely to succeed in life. To be one of these successful persons in the future, one must have at his command a useful, adaptable and highly powerful tool – the English language.

■ The English Sentence – Its Main Parts and Their Functions

Every word in a complete English sentence is a part of speech. To construct a good English sentence, it is necessary that a student of English must be able to recognize easily the eight parts of speech, which are the (1) *nouns*, (2) *pronouns*, (3) *verbs*, (4) *adjectives*, (5) *adverbs*, (6) *prepositions*, (7) *conjunctions* and (8) *interjections*.

▣ Recognizing The Eight Parts of Speech

☐ 1. Noun – A noun (N) expresses the name of persons, places, things, ideas or events.

Persons	Places	Things	Ideas
Digna	Iloilo	wine	celebration
farmer	Mountain	truck	practice

● Classes of Nouns – 1) Proper and 2) Common Nouns

○1) **Proper Nouns** – Proper nouns are *names* of *particular persons, places, things,* or *ideas* written beginning with *capital letters*.

Ex. (*proper nouns* [proper N] = *Paulo, Iloilo City, University of the Philippines, Without Seeing the Dawn, Doctor of Medicine*)

◊ *Darwin* visits *Calinog*.

(name of person, proper N = *Darwin* ; name of place, proper N = *Calinog*)

◊ *Noli Mi Tangere* is a novel written by *Dr. Jose P. Rizal*, our national hero.

(title of book, proper N = Noli Mi Tangere ; name of person, proper N = Dr. Jose P. Rizal

○2) **Common nouns** – Common nouns are *names* of *people, places, things,* or *ideas* written beginning with *small letters*. (*things* or *ideas* may be animals = *gnu* ; objects = *car* ; substances = *water* ; qualities = *courage* ; actions = *loving* ; or measures = kilo)

◊ The *mall* \ is the usual *haunt* of friends.

(name of place, common N = *mall* ; = name of idea, common N = *haunt*

◊ Flashy *cars*, symbolizing *affluence,* / were displayed at the *fair*.

(thing, common N = *cars* ; quality, common N = *affluence* ; place, common N = *fair*)

□ Exercise1 : List down on your paper the *proper* and *common* nouns used in the sentences.

1) Editha visits Liza in Davao every December.

2) Ireneo fought his enemy with valor as a military commander.

3) Nelia is celebrating her birthday this month..

4) Rolly lives in Boracay, which is a village in the town of Malay, Aklan.

5) Erica and Ruth are residents of Pandan.

● Concrete and abstract nouns consist of 1) *tangible* or concrete (can be handled or touched, or pointed to) and 2) *intangible* or *abstract* (cannot be handled or touched, or pointed to, or *ideas* rather than actual things).

o1) *Tangible* or *concrete nouns*

◊ *Malacañang Palace* is the official *residence* of the *President* of the *Philippines*.

◊ The *pen* is mightier than the *sword*.

o2) *Intangible or abstract nouns (ideas)*

◊ *Courage* and *integrity* must be possessed by every person.

◊ Their *honesty* helped them get a *promotion*.

□ Exercise 2 : Identify the *common nouns* in the paragraph.

It is doubtful whether we learn anything from our friends in the way we do from books and study. We do not often observe our friends closely and certainly do not take written notes on what they say. Nevertheless, we do learn from people whom we are close to. From several of my friends, I have learned some important things that I cannot imagine what I would be like, if I had not known them. (*Adapted*)

●Compound nouns are two or more nouns forming a single noun.

o1) Two words joined together = *air* and *port* as in airport ; *base* and *ball* as in baseball ; *jack* and *pot* as in jackpot

o2) Two or more words joined by hyphens = *by* and *line* as in by-line ; *teacher* and *adviser* as in teacher-adviser ; cloak-*and*-dagger ; mother-of-pearl; editor-in-chief

o3) Two words used together, not joined = night owl; branch manager ; Aaron's rod ; pauper's burial

o4)Two or more words used together which are proper nouns = Congress of the Philippines; Bureau of Internat Revenue; Commission on Elections ; Department of Foreign Affairs

● Collective nouns are group of people, places, things or ideas. (Collective nouns = team, herd, committee, Armed Forces of the Philippines, Board of Directors, *etc.,* may be used in the *singular* or *plural* sense)

o1) Singular: ◊ The <u>team</u> / **practices** daily for its final game.

◊ The <u>herd</u> / **was marooned** by the snowstorm.

o2) Plural:

◊ The <u>team</u> / **are discussing** now the strategy to win their last game.

◊ The <u>herd</u> \ **are** a mixture of mature and young goats.

[Note: Symbols used in this discussion are found on page 17.]

☐ Exercise 3 : Write the *nouns* on your paper and indicate whether *proper* or *common*. List down *compound* (*double word*) *nouns* as one. Ex. <u>Daragang Magayon</u>

Bicolanos call their majestic mountain with its near perfect cone Daragang Magayon, meaning Beautiful Maiden. Mayon Volcano, near Legazpi City in Albay, rises to 8,077 feet; its peak is often shrouded in a veil of clouds. A postcard view of the "Fire Mountain" is what tourists most seek from their hotel windows in the port city. (*Adapted*)

☐ Exercise 4 : List down *collective nouns*.

1. The board of directors of the union chose the members of the committee on loans.

2. A pride of lions inhabits the mountainous area.

3. The commission sitting as a whole will decide the petition tomorrow.

4. The chief tasked a panel of interrogators to take over the investigation.

5. The Philippine Army stationed a battalion of soldiers in our town.

● Cases of Nouns – Nouns have three cases: 1) nominative, 2) objective and 3) possessive. (A noun may be nominative or objective; in the possessive case it needs an *apostrophe* (') and letter *s* = ['s].)

o1. Nominative case = 1) subject or 2) predicate noun (PN) of the sentence

1) The <u>judge</u> \ **is** *Joselito Rosales*.

(nominative [subject] = *judge* ; [predicate noun or PN] = *Joselito Rosales*)

2) Senator Aquino \ **is** a *candidate* for President of the Philippines.

        (nominative [subject being named] = *Senator Aquino* ; predicate noun = *candidate*)

o2) Objective case = 1) direct object , 2) indirect objects of verb and 3) object of preposition

    1) Gerry / **commanded** the *battalion*.

    (direct object of the verb **commanded** = *battalion*)

    2) The chief / **named** *Will* the head panelist.

    (indirect object of the verb **named** = *Will* ; direct object = *head panelist*)

    3) Yoly / **sings** at the *club*.

    (object of the preposition *at* = *club* ; sentence has no direct or indirect object)

o 3) Possessive case = noun showing possession; noun ending in 's' doesn't need another 's'

    1) This \ **is** Maris' photograph.

    (The photograph is Maris', not Tess' picture.)

    2) Corazon and Gloria's store / **sells** all kinds of vegetables.

(Only the second noun has an apostrophe and s to show possession.)

    3) My sister-in-law's house / **is situated** in Mandurriao.

    (Hyphenated words show possession with an apostrophe at the end.)

□ Exercise 5 : Identify the *cases* of the *italicized nouns* in the sentences.

1. Alexis is a *chapter president* of a national youth association.

2. Eve and Mikey's *partnership* in business was a model of successful venture.

3. Rando, a panda, tried to outwit the *lion*.

4. Nena runs the show during the *town fiesta*.

5. Eriberto's photograph was reproduced in an *oil painting* by Cesar.

6. Sarah convinced Charlie to sing the *Kundiman* with her.

7. This morning's April rain gently fell on the dry *rice field*.

8. Owen's *car door* jammed and embarrassed him.

9. Teddy is an *architect* of national stature.

10. Intermittent and weak earthquake rocked the city on the onset of a *typhoon*.

☐ Exercise 6 : List down the *nouns* or *noun phrases* found in the paragraphs used as subjects.

Regardless of brand, each cigarette stick / contains at least 43 chemicals that have been linked to cancer. A DoH training manual for its "Healthy Lifestyle" program / says the 43 chemicals form part of over 4,000 toxic substances found in cigarettes. Nitrosamine, crysenes, cadmium, benxol(a)pyrene, polonium 210, nickel, P.A.H., dibenz acidine, B-napthylamine, urethane, N. nitrosonornicotine and toluidine \ are some of these cancer-causing agents.

"Some smokers / think that they reduce the harmful effects of smoking cigarettes by using cigarettes with low tar, low nicotine or filter. This \ is not true," the DoH emphasized. Smokers of low-nicotine cigarettes (less than 1.2 milligrams) / tend to increase the number of sticks they consume to maintain their normal nicotine blood level. (*Adapted*)

☐ Exercise 7 : Identify the *common nouns* in the paragraph.

Marra came to the city with the hope of meeting her long lost half-sister. In the early morning of the next day, she took a taxicab to Mandurriao where Lucille now lives, according to her 75 year-old aunt. When the cab stopped at the gate bearing the address: 1623 Kamagong Drive, Marra had the surprise of her life. Apparently surrounded by brown adobe fence, a mansion of imposing magnificence got her gawking open-mouthed. Does Lucille really live here?

☐ 2. Pronoun - A pronoun (Pron) functions like a noun in the sentence; it takes the place of, or *replaces* a noun, and *identifies* person, place, thing and idea *without renaming* it to avoid monotony.

◊ Paulino **/ had taken** care of *his* baby brother when *his* mother went to the market.

      (person, proper N = *Paulino* ; personal Pron = *his*, identifying Paulino without renaming him)

◊ Denia **/ wrote** a letter to *her* mother.   (person, proper N = *Denia* ; personal Pron = *her*)

◊ Linda \ **is** a singer. *She* trains every day.   (personal Pron = *She*, replacing *Linda*)   ◊ The crowd **/ cheered**. *They* enjoyed the show.   (personal Pron = *They*, replacing *crowd*)

◊ He **/ sings** with *them*. (personal Pron, singular = *He* ; personal Pron, plural = *them*)

◊ Some \ **is** better than *none*.   (personal Pron, indefinite = *Some* ; *none*)

◊ (*Awkward* and *monotonous*) = Dikoy **/ went** to *Dikoy's* farm to get eggs from *Dikoy's* poultry.

◊ (*Correct*) = Dikoy **/ went** to *his* farm to get eggs from *his* poultry.

● Seven classes of pronouns = 1) personal, 2) interrogative, 3) demonstrative, 4) indefinite, 5) relative, 6) reflexive and 7) intensive

   1) *Personal*   = I / **sing** classical songs.   (personal Pron = *I*)

   2) *Interrogative* = Who \ **are** you?   (interrogative Pron = Who)

   3) *Demonstrative* = These \ **are** the books you need. (demonstrative Pron = These)

   4) *Indefinite*   = Some **did not like** catfish.   (indefinite Pron = Some)

5) *Relative*   = Ramy, *who* is a lawyer **/ befriended** Estela. (antecedent of *who* =

  Ramy)

6) *Reflexive* = The teacher, *herself* / **rang** the bell. (The teacher does the work for herself.)

7) *Intensive* = The President, *himself* / **operated** the electric jeepney. (The President draws attention to himself.)

• Personal pronouns have 1) person, 2) number and 3) gender.

1) Person - (1) first person = *person speaking* = We eat to live. I went to Mindanao.

(2) second person = *person spoken to* = You are growing.

(3) third person = *person spoken of* = He sings well. It jumped over the fence.

2) Number - (1) singular = he, she his, hers, I = He entered the academy. I was absent in class.

(2) plural = *we, they, them, us, our, ours, their, theirs (you, your, yours)* = They are big.

3) Gender - (1) masculine = *he, him, his* = His favorite color is green.

(2) feminine = *she, her, hers* = She was the top female performer.

(3) neuter = *it, its* [plural pronouns may be masculine or feminine] = It flies high.

• Personal pronouns have three cases, 1) nominative, 2) objective and 3) possessive cases.

Nominative Objective Possessive   [in bracket = plural form]

First Person   *I, [we] me, [us] my, mine, [our, ours]*
Second Person   *you you, your, yours [your, yours]*
Third Person   *he, she, it, [they] him, her, it, [them]*
                            his, her, hers, its, [their, theirs]

○ (1) Nominative (or Subjective) case pronouns are used as *subjects* of sentences. = *I, we, you, he, she, they, it*

◊ We \ **are** the world.   (nominative Pron; subject of the sentence = We)

◊ He \ is great.   (nominative Pron; subject = He)

◊ She / sings out of tune.   (nominative Pron; subject = She)

◊ They / belong to the aborigines of the islands. (nominative Pron, plural = They)

◊ It / cried because it was hungry.
(nominative Pron, singular = It)

○ In *comparison*, the pronouns are both in the nominative case in the sentence.

◊ *Comparison* = She / sings better than *he*.   (*She* sings better than *he* does.)

◊ Using *who clause* = It \ is I who am knocking at the door. ("It's *me*." is now accepted.)

   = It \ is *who* you know that is important. (*Who* is the person that you know is important?)

◊ *Rejoinder to a statement* = We / want Scotch. I, too. ("*Me*, too." is now correct.)

○(2) Objective case pronouns are used as the *object* of verbs, usually introduced by the preposition *to* ; *to* may be omitted in imperative sentences or when the statement would appear awkward. = *me, us, you, him, her, them, it* ; relative pronouns = *whom a*nd *whomever*

◊ The coach / threw the ball to *him*. (objective Pron = *him*)

◊ / Give this gift to *whomever* gets the highest score.   (objective Pron = *whomever*)

◊ / Give this book to *him*.   (objective Pron = *him*)

◊ / Give *him* this book. (Preposition *to* is omitted.)   (objective Pron = *him*

◊ The judge / sentenced *them* to thirty years of imprisonment. (objective Pron = *them*)

○(3) Possessive case pronouns indicate *possession*. = *my, mine, our, ours, your, yours, his, hers, its, their, theirs*

◊ This \ **is** *my* book.   (possessive Pron, shows book belongs to the speaker = *my*)

◊ *Your* job \ **is** similar to *mine*.   (possessive Pron = *your* ; *mine*)

☐ Exercise 8 : Make a list of the *pronouns* found in the following and indicate their *cases*.

1. Eddie, along with his friends, was arrested by the police of our town.

2. Rodita was requested by her friends to invite their classmates to her birthday party.

3. Normeo's siblings were convinced by their parents to include them in their list of

honorees.

4. Irene was dismayed at her relatives for expecting too much of her.

5. Evelyn told him to avoid seeing Blesilda.

6. – 10. I think I've fully described the beneficial, but unfortunate experience that gave me

insight into my life and myself. My late special grandfather lives in my heart as a guiding light and will be a part of me always. Along with him are my late but inspiringly loving parents.

• 2) Demonstrative pronouns tell which one or group is referred to. (demonstrative pronoun points to a noun after the verb = *this, that, these, those*)

◊ *This* \ **is** the newest *one* and *that* is the oldest in my collection. (referent of *this* = *one*)

◊ *These* \ **are** better *actions* than *those* adopted by the council. (referent of *these* = *actions*)

• 3) Reflexive pronouns signify people performing actions *to, for* and *upon* themselves. (Suffixes –*self* and –*selves* are added to pronouns: first person = *myself, ourselves;* second person = *yourself, yourselves;* third person = *himself, herself, itself, oneself, themselves*)

◊ Surrounded by the police, the bandit / **gave** *himself* up.   (action = for *himself*)

◊ The Orcias / **have bought** *themselves* a boat.   (action = buying boat for *their* own use)

• 4) Intensive pronouns are the same in form as the reflexive pronouns. (intensive Pron draws special attention to the performer of the action.)

◊ The teachers *themselves* / **selected** the school muse. (No other group chose the muse.)

◊ President Ramos *himself* / **drove** the command car during the test. (President Ramos, the Commander-in-Chief, not the aide, drove the command car.)

• 5) Interrogative pronouns begin *questions* = *who, whom, which, what, whose*

◊ *Who* is our national hero?   ◊ *Whose* pencils are these?

• 6) Relative pronouns introduce or start *adjective clauses* which are word groups that modify a word or phrase. The relative pronouns are *who, whom, whose, which* and *that*.

◊ Nikko \ **is** a friend *who raises flowers*. (relative Pron = *who*, introducing adjective clause modifying noun friend = *who raises flowers*)

◊ Ritz / **likes** a dog *that is friendly*. (relative Pron = *that*, introducing adjective clause modifying dog = *that* is friendly)

(Note: Use relative pronoun *who* for *person*, *that* for *thing*, and *which* for *thing* or *idea pinpointed* or *denoted*.)

◊ Corita \ **is** the girl *who* sings off-key.   ◊ The rat *that* ran after the cat / **was killed** by the dog.

◊ He \ is a jolly, good fellow, *which* nobody can deny. (*which* refers to his being a jolly, good fellow)

o *Who* serves as subject of subordinate clause.

14   A Guide in the Study of the Usage of the American English

◊ The <u>person</u> *who answered the phone* \ **was** Jose. (relative Pron, subject of subordinate clause = *who*, introducing subordinate clause = <u>*who* answered the phone</u>

o *Whom* is used in the objective case.

◊ <u>It</u> \ **is** *whom* you know that is important. (You know *whom* that is important.)

o Rule: If there is no other word *before* the verb that could possibly serve as subject of the subordinate clause, then the relative clause is its subject and *who* is correct.

◊ <u>*Who*</u> you know / **can help** you get a job. (Who can help you get a job?)

o Antecedents or referents of pronouns are the nouns that the pronouns refer to, or that the pronouns replace or take the places of.

◊ <u>Lino</u> / **did not know** *it* was *his* dog *that* stuck *its* paw in a pail of glue. (referent or antecedent of *his* = <u>Lino</u> ; referent of *it* and *its* = *dog* ; relative Pron = *that*, introducing adjective clause = <u>*that* stuck its paw</u> in a pail of glue)

• 7) Indefinite pronouns refer to people, places and things in general, without antecedents or referents and most are singular in usage:

all, both, few, none, several, another, each, many, nothing,   some any, either, more, no one, somebody, anybody, everybody, most, one,   someone, anyone, everyone, neither, other   something,   anything, everything, nobody, plenty

◊ <u>*Many*</u> \ **are** called, but *few* are chosen.   (indefinite Pron = *many, few*)

◊ <u>*Something*</u> \ **is** always better than *nothing*. (indefinite Pron = *something, nothing*)

□ Exercise 9 : Choose the correct *pronoun* or *pronouns*.

1. The nominative pronouns are (*I, we, you, they, he, she* and *it* \ *us, me, him, her* and *them*).

2. *You* and (*I* \ *me*) can study together.

3. Bert and (*he* \ *him*) refereed the basketball game.

4. He never saw the Lazaros or (*they* \ *them*).

5. The police mistook (*him* \ *he*) for (*me* \ *I*).

6. (*Us* \ *We*) boys were better than (*they* \ *them*) were.

7. Any player (*who* \ *whom*) Oscar can beat must be ill-prepared.

8. It is (*who* \ *whom*) you know that is important.

9. This is (*any* \ *something*) for you and (*me* \ *I*) to think about.

10. People (*who* \ *whom*) are honest themselves usually trust others.

☐ 3. Verb - A verb (V) expresses *action* or *state of being*.

• An *action verb* (AV) describes the *action* or *movement* of someone or something that is either *physical* or *mental*.

  ○ *Physical action* = Tony / **drives** fast cars.   (action verb or AV, physical = **drives**)

  = Perla / **reads** magazines.   (action verb or AV, physical = **reads**)

  ○ *Mental action* = Delilah / **thinks** she has a pleasant disposition. (AV, mental = **thinks**)

  = Carmen / **expects** to succeed as an actress.   (AV, mental = **expects**)

• A *state of being verb* (SOBV) or linking verb (LV) shows the condition or state of existence of someone or something. Linking verbs **am, is, are, was,** and **were** connect complements or completers to the subjects of the sentence. Complements or completers identify or describe the subjects.

◊ The hero \ is dead.   (*be* verb = **is**, linking verb [LV] ; completer [Adj] = *dead*)

◊ She \ is a doctor. (LV = **is**, connecting *doctor* [completer] to subject = She)

• *Auxiliary* or *helping verbs* (HV) are verbs *to be* or *be* verbs in verb phrases used to express time. The helping verb (HV) group includes action verbs *do* and *have*, and *modals*. (See page 18)

1) *Be*: **am, is, are, was, were, be, being, been**

2) _Do_: **does, do, did**

3) _Have_: **has, have, had**

4) _Modals_: **can, could, may, might, must, ought, shall, should, will, would**

● The *action* verbs *helped* by *auxiliary* verbs (HV) are called *main verbs* (MV), which are in the participle form, and together, they form the *action verb phrases* (AV phrases).

◊ Megan / **is singing** happily on her birthday.

(present progressive time AV phrase [**HV** + **MV**] = **is singing**; helping verb

[HV] = **is**; main verb [MV] = **singing**)

◊ The bell / **was sounded** dolefully.

(past time AV phrase [**HV** + **MV**] = **was sounded**; HV, past time = **was**; MV, past

participle = **sounded**)

◊ Luz / **will pass** the acid test to come out the winner.

(future time AV phrase [**HVM** + **MV**] = **will pass**; modal [HVM] = **will**, serving as

HV; main verb [MV], present time = **pass**)

● The action verb (AV) **have** is used as helping verb (HV) only in *perfect time verb phrases*

◊ The province / **has** no governor. (AV, present time for singular N subject = **has**)

◊ Governor Marcial and Vice Governor Isla / **have resigned**. (present perfect time

AV phrase [**HV** + **MV**] = **have resigned**; HV, present time = **have**; MV, past time

[participle] = **resigned**)

◊ The swimming team / **has won** four gold medals. (AV phrase, present perfect time [

HV + MV] = **has won**; HV, present time = **has**; MV, past participle = **won**)

- *Do, does* and *did* also function as helping verbs in *emphatic* and *interrogative verb phrases.*

◊ Rupert / **does sing** the Kundiman.   (*emphatic* present time AV phrase [**HV + MV**] =

        does sing; HV, present time = **does**; MV, present time = **sing**)

◊ **Did** Sylvia **invite** her sister to her wedding? (past time *interrogative AV phrase,*[**HV + MV**] = **did invite**; HV, past time = **did**; MV, present time = **invite**) [Note: In interrogative sentence, the subject (SN) is inserted in the verb phrase: **did invite** = **did** Sylvia **invite**]

☐ 4. Adjective - An adjective (Adj) describes or modifies nouns or pronouns by giving "color" to make them more specific. Below are some nouns being "colored" by adjectives. An adjective answers any one of the following questions: *What kind? Which one? How many? How much?*

◊ Efren / **wears** a *blue* shirt.   (*What kind of shirt?* = *blue*, Adj, modifying N = shirt)

◊ Aiza / **owns** *that* car.   (*Which car?* = *that*, Adj, modifying N = car)

◊ They/ **bought** *five* houses.   (*How many?* = *five*, Adj, modifying N = houses)

◊ The athletes / **need** *more* practice.   (*How much?*]= *more*, Adj, modifying N = practice)

- An adjective following a linking verb (LV) is known as adjective complement and is referred to as *predicate adjective* (PA); this adjective *modifies* the subject noun or completes the idea *describing* the subject. (Sentence Pattern: S + LV + Adj)

◊ The car \ **is** *old*.   (LV = **is**; predicate adjective or PA = *old*)

◊ The lady \ **is** a *doctor*.   (The noun following a linking verb is called predicate noun

[PN]. [Sentence Pattern: S + LV + N] ; predicate noun [PN] = *doctor*)

☐ 5. Adverb - An adverb (Adv) modifies 1) a *verb*, 2) an *adjective* or 3) another *adverb*.

◊ 1) Kaya Sharly **/ speaks** English *fluently*. (Adv = *fluently*, modifying AV = **speaks**)

◊ 2) They **\ are** *very* fluent English speakers. (Adv = *very*, modifying Adj [PA} = fluent)

◊ 3) Edda Mae **/ speaks** English *quite* fluently. (Adv = *quite*, [also called *intensifie*r],

modifying another Adv = *fluently*)

. • Adverbs answer questions *When? How? Where? Why? How much? How little? To what extent?*

◊ Adv of time (*when?*) = He **/ arrived** *today*. (Adv = *today*, modifying AV = **arrived**)

◊ Adv of manner (*how?*) = Vince **/ drives** *carefully*. (Adv = *carefully*, modifying AV = **drives**)

◊ Adv of place (*where?*) = Merryl **/ is working** *here*. (Adv = *here*, modifying AV = **is working**)

◊ Adv of cause (*why?*) = We **/ met**, *because we want to form an association*. (Adv [dependent clause] = *because we want to form an association*, modifying AV = **met**

◊ Adv of degree (*to what extent?*) = The weather **\ was** *extremely* cold. Adv = *extremely*, modifying predicate Adj [PA] = *cold*; *extremely cold* complementing LV = **was**

☐ 6. Preposition - A preposition (Prep) expresses relationship between nouns or pronouns and other words in sentences.

◊ Three books **\ are** *on* the table. (Prep = *on*, telling the relationship of *books* and *table*, or telling where the books are in relation to the table = [*on* the table])

◊ The fountain pen **\ is** *in* the table drawer. (Prep = *in*) o The noun or pronoun following the preposition is called the *object of the preposition.*

◊ Deep sea <u>divers</u> **/ find** pearls *beneath* the <u>sea</u>. (*Prep = beneath*; object of *Prep = sea*)

◊ What the scientist told his audience \ **is** *beyond* <u>him</u>. (*Prep = beyond*; object of *Prep = him*)

o List of some prepositions (*compound prepositions* consist. of more than one word):

Above behind   down near since   according to   in place of
about   below   during   of   through   as   of   with
regard to across   beneath   except off   till   as well as in
spite of against   beside   for   into   to   by means of in
accord with along besides from   onto   toward in front of out
of around between   in   out   under   prior to as regards to at
                by   inside   outside with   before despite like over
within

◊ The <u>theater</u> \ **stands** *in front of* the cultural center.   (compound *Prep = in front of*;

 object of *Prep* = center)

◊ The <u>dictionary</u> \ **is** *in* the shelf. (Prep phrase, completer = *in the shelf* (*in* = preposition expressing where the dictionary is in relation to the shelf)

☐ 7. Conjunction - A conjunction (Conj) connects individual words or group of words.

◊ <u>Science</u> *and* <u>technology</u> **/ proved** to be both boon *and* bane to man. (Conj = *and*, connecting N = *science* to another N = *technology*; another conj = *and*, connecting

   N = *boon*, to another N = *bane*

◊ <u>We</u> **/ must reforest** denuded mountains *or* <u>we</u> **/ will make** a desert of our earth.

(Conj = *or*, connecting two clauses beginning with Pron = we)

o Three kinds of conjunctions: 1) *coordinating*, 2) *correlative* and 3) *subordinating conjunctions*

o 1) *Coordinating* (coord) conjunctions connect similar parts of speech or words performing the same functions. (coordinating Conj = *and, but, for, nor, or, so, yet*)

◊ She \ **is** beautiful, rich *and* intelligent. (coord Conj = *and*, joining the Adj = *beautiful, rich* and *intelligent*, being words of equal rank)

◊ Brian *and* Val / **study** Mathematics, Science *and* English every night. (coord Conj = *and*, connecting proper N = Brian and Val and Science *and* English)

◊ Much / **was expected** of him, *so* Franco / **did** his best. (coord Conj = *so*, connecting two independent clauses)

◊ Karen / **went** to the airport to get an incoming package *and* to welcome her cousin.

(coord Conj = *and*, connecting two verbal phrases)

o 2) *Correlative* conjunctions consist of two or more words that work together as a set. Correlative and coordinating conjunctions connect words that perform equal functions in a sentence.

either ... or ...whether ... or ...neither ... nor ...   not only ... but (also) ...   both ... and ...

◊ The team / **had** *both* mettle *and* inspiration. (correlative Conj = *both ... and ...*, connecting mettle, inspiration)

o 3) *Subordinating* conjunctions (subord Conj) connect words to show unequal, but important relationships between certain ideas by making one of the ideas subordinate or dependent on the other. In a complex sentence, a subordinating conjunction connects a subordinate clause to a main or independent clause.

◊ The villagers / **organized** a cooperative, *because* they wanted progress. (subord Conj

= *because*, connecting the subordinate clause = *because they want progress* to the independent clause = *The villagers organized a cooperative*.)

○ Subordinating conjunctions express relationship of time, manner, cause, condition, comparison, or purpose. *Conjunctive adverb* is the other term for subordinating conjunction.

Time MannerCause Condition Comparison Purpose after as because although as in order that as as if as long as than so that as long as although even if that as soon as even though before if since provided that until, till through

When where unless

whenever wherever while

while whereas now that inasmuch as

☐ 8. Interjection - An interjection (Interj) is a special word, phrase or clause that expresses sudden emotions and can stand alone by itself, although it may appear as part of a sentence. The punctuation mark used for the expression is an exclamation point.

◊ *Congratulations!* (*Interj* = a sentence by itself expressing a strong feeling)

◊ *Hooray! We won!* (*Interj* = a single-word sentence plus a sentence of several words)

◊ *Help*! We're being robbed!

○ Some interjectory words:

Ah alas gee whiz gracious

hey oh psst

well whoa aha

dear goodness   help hooray

ouch tsk tsk   whew wow

◘ The Structure of the English Sentence

● The study of the eight parts of speech, namely, noun, pronoun, verb, adjective, adverb. preposition, conjunction and interjection, requires the understanding of the eight parts of speech in a sentence. The sentence will be parsed to some practical extent as a step to make things clear to high school students. Discussions that appear repetitive are not just repetitions, but reiterative ways to enable the slow learners to gain a useful knowledge of the English grammar. The high school students must understand how the most important part of speech -- the *verb* or *verb phrase* -- is used along with the *subject noun phrase*. Among the eight parts of speech, the verb and its function is the most complicated and difficult to understand.

- The *sentence* is *a word or group of words* that *expresses a complete thought or meaning*. A one-word sentence has its first letter capitalized; if the sentence consists of several words, the first letter of the first word is capitalized. The English sentence is ended by a terminal punctuation: a period (.) for declarative (statement) and imperative sentences; a question mark (?) for an interrogative sentence (question) and an exclamation point (!) for an expression of strong feeling (exclamatory sentence).

1) *One-word sentences*
   ◊ Good. (Declarative)
   ◊ Sing. (Imperative)
   ◊ Why? (Interrogative)
   ◊ Wow! (Exclamatory)

2) *Sentence made up of several words* ◊ The weather is fine. (Declarative)

3) *Sentences ending in a period* ◊ This car is mine. (Declarative)
   ◊ You may go. (Imperative)

4) *Sentences ending in a question mark* ◊ Did you pass the test? (Interrogative)
   ◊ What did you do? (Interrogative)

5) *Sentences ending in an exclamation point* ◊ Help! Help! (Exclamatory)
   ◊ Our house is on fire! (Exclamatory)

- The *sentence* is made up of *two main parts* or *groups of words*, which are 1) the *complete subject* or *subject noun phrase* (S) and 2) the *complete predicate* or *verb phrase* (V). These two parts are separated from each other by a bar, as indicated (Refer to the identifying symbols used).

○ Complete sentence = <u>My mother</u> / **cooks** food for the family.

◊ 1) *complete subject* (SN) = <u>My *mother*</u>

◊ 2) *complete predicate* (V or AV) = **cooks** food for the family

● 1) The *complete subject (subject noun phrase) tells who or what the sentence is about.* The *simple subject* is *mother*, (as shown in *italics*); <u>My *mother*</u> is also called the *subject noun phrase* (SN).

● 2) The *complete predicate (verb phrase)* tells *what someone or something does, did* or *is* or *was.* The *simple predicate* or *verb* (V) is **cooks**, while the complete *predicate* or *complete verb phrase* is <u>**cooks** food for the family</u>.

(1)   <u>Eddie</u> **/ operates** a fleet of taxicabs. (what someone *does* [AV] = **operates**)

(2)   <u>Rida</u> / **sent** a letter to her cousin.   (what someone *did* [AV]= **sent**)

(3)   <u>Nitz</u> \ **is** the wife of a senator.   (what someone *is* [LV] = **is**)

(4)   <u>Ed</u> \ **was** an instructor in school.   (what someone *was* [LV]= **was**)

● The *complete subject* of a sentence may consist of *one word only* (*noun* or *pronoun*); however, it is referred to as a *subject noun phrase* (SN or SPron); the *complete predicate*, which may also be one word, may also be called a *verb phrase* (V or AV).

o A one-word sentence is usually an imperative verb that gives *command, order,* or *request.* The single-word sentence group includes *expression* of *comments* or *remarks, follow-up questions* and *answers.* Examples of single words which are also complete sentences: imperative verbs *Go. Sing.*; questions or answers *Why?Me?You? How? Yes. No.* ; comments or interjections *Good. Excellent, Okay, Bravo, Congratulations!* and expletives or adverbs *There. Here.,* etc.

□ Exercise 10 : Separate the *complete subject* and the *complete predicate* of the sentence by copying on your paper the words comprising the two parts (the complete subject on the first line and the complete predicate on the succeeding line).

    1. Ruping, a very strong typhoon, destroyed many houses.

    2. One cold December morning, Rosendo went up the mountain.

3. The mayor was disappointed by the action of the city council.

4. Some policemen were commended for bravery posthumously.

5. Easily cutting across the plains, the safari crossed the turbulent river before the rains.

6. No one here is Simon Peter?

7. Rarely ill in ninety years, her grandfather died on her wedding day.

8. Erica lost her valuables to the fire that gutted their house.

9. The candidate for Miss Dinagyang did not win despite spending a big amount of money.

10. After having been sent to prison for murder, Celso reformed and became a Baptist minister.

o In studying the various parts of the sentence, there is a need to mark or identify each part by the use of letter symbols. The identifying symbols used here are as follows:

Noun = *noun* or *noun* phrase or subject = N or SN

Pron = *pronoun* or subject pronoun = Pron or SPron

V = *verb* or *verb phrase*

AV = action verb

SOBV = state of being verb

LV = linking verb

MV = main verb

HV = helping verb

MHV = main helping verb

HVM = helping verb modal

\ = separating LV and SN or SPron

/ = separating AV and SN or SPron

= indicating or pointing sign

v. i. = verb, intransitive

v. t. = verb, transitive
Adv = *adverb*
Adj = *adjective*
Conj = *conjunction*
Prep = *preposition*
Interj = *interjection*
O / DO = object / direct object
IO = indirect object
OC = objective complement

☐ Noun or Noun Phrase – Its Composition as Subject of the Sentence

● A noun exists in the form of a phrase called *noun phrase* (N) that serves as the *subject* of the sentence (SN). The *subject noun phrase* (SN) may be 1a) a *single word (noun)*, 1b) *several words (nouns)*, or 2) a *pronoun* (SPron), 3) a *noun* with a *determiner* and / or 3a) a *noun* with a *determiner* and *predeterminer*, or 4) an *adjective*, functioning as a noun.

  o 1a) Single word as (1) *singular subject noun* or SN = Maya; (2) *plural noun* as SN = girls

◊ (1) Maya / **sings**.   ◊ (2) Girls / **dance** the Tinikling.
         ↑   ↑
  SN, singular = Maya   SN, plural = girls

  o 1b) Several words as *singular subject noun* or SN = My brother Roberto

◊ My brother Roberto / **planted** mango trees.
            ↑
  SN, singular = *Roberto*; appositive = *My brother*, identifying *Roberto*

  o 2) *Singular subject pronoun* or SPron = she; *plural subject pronoun* or SPron = they

◊ She / **dances**.   ◊ They / **study** engineering.
      ↑   ↑
  SPron, singular = she   SPron, plural = they

○ 3) *Subject noun* with *determiner*, a definite article = *The* girl
◊ *The* girl / **wrote** a poem.

    ↑ *The* = determiner

    SN, singular = girl

○ 3a) *Subject noun phrase* with a *predeterminer* (SPron) + *determiners* = Few *of the fifty* carabaos; (Few, the predeterminer, a *pronoun*, is the subject of the sentence; not *carabao*.)

◊ Few *of the fifty* carabaos / **are wandering** in the forest.
 ↑ ↑ ↑

      N = *carabaos*, object of Prep = *of*
predeterminer, ——— determiners = *the* and *fifty* (part of the prepositional phrase Adj = SPron, plural = few *of the fifty carabaos*, modifying plural SPron = few)

○ 4) *Adjective as subject of the sentence,* when the noun is not necessary to stress the obvious.

◊ The poor \ **are** patient people. (The poor people \ **are** patient.)

   ↑

  SN, plural (Adj) = poor, *adjective in the phrase* = *poor* people

◊ The wounded / **were treated** by doctors.

   ↑

  SN, plural = wounded (Adj), past participle of AV = **wound**) in the phrase = *wounded* men

◊ (Note: To: All Concerned:, an official memo address/greeting, *concerned* is the past participle of the verb *concern* used as a noun ; [Adj, as in the phrase *concerned teachers*])

☐ Determiner and Predeterminer in a Noun Phrase

● The *determiner* is an *adjective* which signals that a *noun* is coming; it is also called a *noun marker* or *marker.* The four kinds of determiners are

1) *articles*, 2) *pointing* or *demonstrative pronouns*, 3) *possessive pronouns* and 4) *numbers*. A determiner functions as *adjective* in the sentence.

- 1) *Articles* = *a, an* and *the*
  - ◊ *A* hen / **laid** two-dozen eggs. (indefinite article = a)
  - ◊ *An* orange / **dropped** from the tree. (indefinite article = a*n*)
  - ◊ *The* bougainvilleas / **were planted** last year. (definite article = *the*)
- 2) *Pointing Pronouns or Demonstratives* = *this, these, that* and *those*
  - ◊ *This* book \ **is** our reference. (singular = *this*)
  - ◊ *These* trees / **were knocked** down during the storm. (plural = *these*)
  - ◊ *That* girl \ **is** Junjie's friend. (singular = *that*)
  - ◊ *Those* cars / **arrived** yesterday from Malaysia. (plural = those)
- 3) *Possessives* = *her, hers, his, my, mine, our, ours, your, yours, their, theirs,* and *its*
  - ◊ *Her* racquet / **was broken** during practice. (*her*)
  - ◊ The gift brought by Cielo \ **is** *hers* and not *mine*. (*hers, mine*)
  - ◊ *Our* program / **did not push** through because of the rain. (our)
- 4) *Numbers* = *three, few, many, some, a hundred, ten thousand . . .* etc.
  - ◊ *Three* coins / **were dropped** in the fountain.
  - ◊ *Many* men / **are called** but *few* / **are chosen**.

- Determiners and Predeterminers – The *determiner* is an *adjective* serving as a *noun marker giving signal that a noun is coming.* The *predeterminer* is a *pronoun*, like *many, some, several*, etc., serving as the *simple subject* of the sentence and the verb agrees with it.

  ◊ Many of the forty students \ **were** absent.

  ↑   ↑ ↑   N = *students*, object of Prep = *of*
  predeterminer, ——— determiners (the, forty)

  (SPron, plural) = many [complete subject noun phrase or SPron, plural] = Many *of the forty students* ; predeterminer serving as the subject of the sentence = <u>many</u> ; prepositional phrase = *of the forty students* as Adj modifying <u>many</u> ; linking verb [LV] agreeing with <u>many</u> = **were**)

◊ <u>Several</u> *of our five flashlights* / **need** new batteries.

= *of* predeterminer,   N = *flashlights*, object of Prep determiners (our, five)

(SPron, plural) = <u>Several,</u> [predeterminer used as subject of the sentence] ; prepositional phrase Adj, modifying <u>several</u> = *of our five flashlights* ; possessive Pron as Adj modifying *flashlight* = *our* ; action verb [AV} agreeing with <u>Several</u> = **need**)

□ Verb or Verb Phrase and Its Forms as Predicate of the Sentence

• Verbs are grouped into three: 1) the *Action* Verbs, 2) the *State of Being* Verbs or *Linking* Verbs and 3) the *Auxiliary* or *Helping* Verbs.

□ 3. Verb - A verb (V) expresses *action* or *state of being.*

• An *action verb* (AV) describes the *action* or *movement* of someone or something that is either *physical* or *mental.*

○ *Physical action* = Rene / **drives** fast cars.   (action verb or AV, physical = **drives**)

= They / **read** magazines.   (action verb or AV, physical = **read**)

○ *Mental action* = <u>Delia</u> / **thinks** she has a pleasant disposition. (AV, mental = **thinks**)

= His mom / **wanted** him to succeed as an actor. (AV, mental = **wanted**)

• A *state of being verb* (SOBV) or simply *state verb* is also called a *linking verb* (LV). *State verb* shows the condition or state of existence of someone or something. Linking verbs **am, is, are, was,** and **were** connect complements or completers to the subjects of the sentence. Complements or completers identify or describe the subjects.

◊ The hero \ <u>is</u> dead.   (*be* verb = **is**, linking verb [LV] ; completer [Adj] = *dead*)

◊ She \ **is** a doctor.   (LV = **is**, connecting *doctor* [completer] to subject = She)

• *Auxiliary* or *helping verbs* (HV) are verbs *to be* or *be* verbs in verb phrases used to express time. The helping verb (HV) group includes action verbs *do* and *have*, and *modals*. (See p. 18)

1) *Be*: **am, is, are, was, were, be, being, been**

2) *Do*: **does, do, did**

3) *Have*: **has, have, had**

4) *Modals*: **can, could, may, might, must, ought, shall, should, will, would**

• The *action* verbs *helped* by *auxiliary* verbs (HV) are called *main verbs* (MV), which are in the participle form, and together, they form the *action verb phrases* (AV phrases).

◊ Megan / is singing happily on her birthday.

(present progressive time AV phrase [**HV** + **MV**] = **is singing**; helping verb [HV] = **is**; main verb [MV] = **singing**)

◊ The bell / was sounded dolefully.

(past time AV phrase [**HV** + **MV**] = **was sounded**; HV, past time = **was**; MV,

past participle = **sounded**)

◊ Luz / will pass the acid test to come out the winner.

(future time AV phrase [**HVM** + **MV**] = **will pass**; modal [HVM] = **will**, serving as HV; main verb [MV], present time = **pass**)

• The action verb (AV) **have** is used as helping verb (HV) only in *perfect time verb phrases*

◊ The province / **has** no governor.   (AV, present time for singular N subject = **has**)

◊ Governor Marcial and Vice_Governor Isla / **have resigned**. (present perfect time

    AV phrase [**HV + MV**] = **have resigned**; HV, present time = **have**; MV, past time [participle] = **resigned**)

◊ The swimming team / **has won** four gold medals.   AV phrase, present perfect time

    [**HV + MV**] = **has won**; HV, present time = **has**; MV, past participle = **won**)

• *Do, does* and *did* also function as helping verbs in *emphatic* and *interrogative verb phrases.*

    ◊ Rupert / **does sing** the Kundiman.   (*emphatic* present time *AV phrase* [**HV + MV**] =

    does sing; HV, present time = **does;** MV, present time = **sing**)

◊ **Did** Martha **invite** her sister to her wedding? (past time *interrogative AV phrase,*[**HV +**

    MV] = **did invite**; HV, past time = **did**; MV, present time = **invite**)

☐ 4. Adjective - An adjective (Adj) describes or modifies nouns or pronouns by giving "color" to make them more specific. Below are some nouns being "colored" by adjectives. An adjective answers any one of the following questions: *What kind? Which one? How many?* or *How much?*

◊ Efren / **wears** a *blue* shirt.   (*What kind of shirt?* = *blue,* Adj, modifying N = shirt)

◊ Aiza / **owns** *that* car.   (*Which car?* = *that,* Adj, modifying N = car)

◊ They/ **bought** *five* houses.   (*How many?* = *five,* Adj, modifying N = houses)

◊ The athletes / **need** *more* practice.   (*How much?*]= *more,* Adj, modifying N = practice)

- An adjective following a linking verb (LV) is known as adjective complement and is referred to as *predicate adjective* (PA); this adjective *modifies* the subject noun or completes the idea *describing* the subject. (Sentence Pattern: S + LV + Adj)

◊ The <u>car</u> \ **is** *old.* (LV = **is**; predicate adjective or PA = *old*)

◊ The <u>lady</u> \ **is** a *doctor.* (The noun following a linking verb is called predicate noun

[PN]. [Sentence Pattern: S + LV + N] ; predicate noun [PN] = *doctor*)

☐ 5. Adverb - An adverb (Adv) modifies 1) a *verb*, 2) an *adjective* or 3) another *adverb*.

◊ 1) Kaya Sharly / **speaks** English *fluently.* (Adv = *fluently*, modifying AV = **speaks**)

◊ 2) <u>They</u> \ **are** <u>very</u> *fluent* English speakers. (Adv = <u>very</u>, modifying Adj [PA} =

fluent)

◊ 3) <u>Eda Mae</u> / **speaks** English <u>quite</u> *fluently.* (Adv = <u>quite</u>, [also called *intensifie*r], modifying another Adv = *fluently*]

- Adverbs answer questions *When?, How?, Where?, Why?, How much?* or *How little?* or *To what extent?*

◊ Adv of time (*when?*) = <u>He</u> / **arrived** *today.* (Adv = *today*, modifying AV = **arrived**)

◊ Adv of manner (*how?*) = <u>Vince</u> / **drives** *carefully.* (Adv = *carefully*, modifying AV = **drives**)

◊ Adv of place (*where?*) = <u>Merryl</u> / **is working** *here.* (Adv = *here*, modifying AV = **is working**)

◊ Adv of cause (*why?*) = <u>We</u> / **met**, *because we want to form an association.*

(Adv [dependent clause] = *because we want to form an association*, modifying

AV = **met**

◊ Adv of degree (*to what extent?*) = The <u>weather</u> \ **was** *extremely* cold. (Adv = *extremely*, modifying predicate Adj [PA] = *cold*; *extremely cold* complementing LV = **was**

☐ 6. Preposition - A preposition (Prep) expresses relationship between nouns or pronouns and other words in sentences.

◊ Three <u>books</u> \ **are** *on* the table. (Prep = *on*, telling the relationship of *books* and *table*, or telling where the books are in relation to the table [*on* the table])

◊ The <u>fountain pen</u> \ **is** *in* the table drawer. (Prep = *in*)

○ The noun or pronoun following the preposition is called the *object of the preposition*.

◊ Deep sea <u>divers</u> / **find** pearls *beneath* the sea. (*Prep* = *beneath*; object of *Prep* = *sea*)

◊ What the scientist told his audience \ **is** *beyond* him. (*Prep* = *beyond*; object of *Prep* = *him*)

○ List of some prepositions (*compound prepositions* consist. of more than one word):

Above behind down near since according to in place of

About below during of through as of with regard to

Across beneath except off till as well as in spite of

Against beside for into to by means of

in accord with along besides from onto toward in front of

out of

around between in out under prior to as regards to

at by inside outside with before despite

like over within

◊ The <u>theater</u> \ **stands** *in front of* the cultural center. (compound *Prep* = in front of;

object of *Prep* = center)

◊ The dictionary \ is *in* the shelf. (Prep phrase, completer = *in the shelf* (*in* = preposition expressing where the dictionary is in relation to the shelf)

☐ 7. Conjunction - A conjunction (Conj) connects individual words or group of words.

◊ Science *and* technology **/ proved** to be both boon *and* bane to man. (Conj = *and*, connecting N = *science* to another N = *technology*; another conj = *and*, connecting N = *boon*, to another N = *bane*

◊ We **/ must reforest** denuded mountains *or* we **/ will make** a desert of our earth.

(Conj = *or*, connecting two clauses beginning with Pron = we)

o Three kinds of conjunctions: 1) *coordinating*, 2) *correlative* and 3) *subordinating conjunctions*

o 1) *Coordinating* (coord) conjunctions connect similar parts of speech or words performing the same functions. (coordinating Conj = *and, but, for, nor, or, so, yet*)

◊ She \ **is** beautiful, rich *and* intelligent. (coord Conj = *and*, joining the Adj = *beautiful, rich* and *intelligent,* being words of equal rank)

◊ Brian *and* Val **/ study** Mathematics, Science *and* English every night.(coord Conj = *and*, connecting proper N = Brian and Val and Science *and* English)

◊ Much **/ was expected** of him, *so* Franco **/ did** his best. (coord Conj = *so*, connecting two independent clauses)

◊ Karen **/ went** to the airport to get an incoming package *and* to welcome her cousin.

coord Conj = *and*, connecting two verbal phrases)

o 2) *Correlative* conjunctions consist of two or more words that work together as a set. Correlative and coordinating conjunctions connect words that perform equal functions in a sentence.

either … or …whether … or …neither … nor …   not only … but (also) …   both … and …

◊ The team / had *both* mettle *and* inspiration. (correlative Conj = *both … and …*,

connecting mettle, inspiration)

o 3) *Subordinating* (subord) conjunctions connect words to show unequal but important relationships between certain ideas by making one of the ideas subordinate or dependent on the other. In a complex sentence, a subordinating conjunction connects a subordinate clause to a main or independent clause.

◊ The villagers / **organized** a cooperative, *because* they wanted progress. (subord Conj

= *because*, connecting the subordinate clause = *because they want progress* to the independent clause = *The villagers organized a cooperative.*)

o Subordinating conjunctions express relationship of time, manner, cause, condition, comparison, or purpose. *Conjunctive adverb* is the other term for subordinating conjunction.

Time	Manner	Cause	Condition	Compariso n	Purpose
After	As	because	although	as	in order that
As		as if	As long as	than	so that
as long as		although	even if	that	
as soon as		even though			
Before		if			
Since		provided that			

until, till		through			
When	Where	unless			
whenever	Wherever	while			
while		whereas	now that		inasmuch as

☐ 8. Interjection - An interjection (Interj) is a special word, phrase or clause that expresses sudden emotions and can stand alone by itself, although it may appear as part of a sentence. The punctuation mark used for the expression is an exclamation point.

◊ *Congratulations!*   (*Interj* = a sentence by itself expressing a strong feeling)

◊ *Hooray! We won!*   (*Interj* = a single-word sentence plus a sentence of several words)

◊ *Help*! We're being robbed!

o Some interjectory words:

Ah alas gee whiz gracious hey   oh
                                  psst
                             well whoa
Aha dear goodness help hooray ouch tsk tsk whew wow

The English Sentence Structure And Its Two Main Parts

● The *sentence* is made up of *two main parts* or *groups of words*, which are 1) the *complete subject* or *subject noun phrase* (S) and 2) the *complete predicate* or *verb phrase* (V). These two parts are separated from each other by a bar, as indicated (Refer to the identifying symbols used).

  ○ Complete sentence = <u>My *mother*</u> **/ cooks** food for the family.

   ◊ 1) *complete subject* (SN) = <u>My *mother*</u>

   ◊ 2) *complete predicate* (V or AV) = **cooks** food for the family

● 1) The *complete subject* (*subject noun phrase*) *tells who or what the sentence is about*. The *simple subject* is <u>*mother*</u>, (as shown in *italics*); <u>My *mother*</u> is also called the *subject noun phrase* (SN).

● 2) The *complete predicate* (*verb phrase*) tells *what someone or something does, did* or *is* or *was*. The *simple predicate* or *verb* (V) is **cooks**, while the complete *predicate* or *complete verb phrase* is **cooks** <u>food for the family</u>.

<u>Eddie</u> **/ operates** a fleet of taxicabs. (what someone *does* [AV] = **operates**)

- <u>Aida</u> **/ sent** a letter to her cousin. (what someone *did* [AV]= **sent**)
- <u>She</u> \ **is** the wife of a senator. (what someone *is* [LV] = **is**)
- <u>He</u> \ **was** an instructor in school. (what someone *was* [LV]= **was**)

● The *complete subject* of a sentence may consist of *one word only* (*noun* or *pronoun*); however, it is referred to as a *subject noun phrase* (SN or SPron); the *complete predicate*, which may also be one word, may also be called a *verb phrase* (V or AV).

  ○ A one-word sentence is usually an imperative verb that gives *command, order,* or *request*. The single-word sentence group includes *expression* of *comments* or *remarks, follow-up questions* and *answers*. Examples of single words which are also complete sentences: imperative verbs *Go., Sing.*; questions or answers *Why?, How? Yes. No.* ; comments or interjections *Good. Excellent. Okay, Bravo, Congratulations* and expletives or adverbs *There. Here.*, etc.

□ Noun or Noun Phrase – Its Composition as Subject of the Sentence

● A noun exists in the form of a phrase called *noun phrase* (N) that serves as the *subject* of the sentence (SN). The *subject noun phrase* (SN) may be 1a) a *single word (noun)*, 1b) *several words (nouns)*, or 2) a *pronoun* (SPron), 3) a *noun* with a *determiner* and / or 3a) a *noun* with a *determiner* and *predeterminer*, or 4) an *adjective*, functioning as a noun.

○ 1a) Single word as (1) *singular subject noun* or SN = Maya; (2) *plural noun* as SN = girls

◊ (1) Maya **/ sings**.   ◊ (2) Girls **/ dance** the Tinikling.
    ↑   ↑
SN, singular = Maya   SN, plural = girls

1b) Several words as *singular subject noun* or SN = My brother Roberto

◊ My brother Roberto **/ planted** mango trees.
        ↑
        SN, singular = *Roberto*; appositive = *My brother*, identifying *Roberto*

○ 2) *Singular subject pronoun* or SPron = she; *plural subject pronoun* or SPron = they

◊ She **/ dances**.   ◊ They **/ study** engineering.
   ↑   ↑
SPron, singular = she   SPron, plural = they

○ 3) *Subject noun* with *determiner*, a definite article = *The* girl

◊ *The* girl **/ wrote** a poem.
     ↑   ↑_____ SN, singular = girl

determiner = *the*

○ 3a) *Subject noun phrase* with a *predeterminer* (SPron) + *determiners* = <u>Few</u> *of the fifty* carabaos; (<u>Few</u>, the predeterminer, a *pronoun*, is the subject of the sentence; not *carabao*.)

◊ <u>Few</u> *of the fifty* carabaos / **are wandering** in the forest.

↑ ↑ ↑   N = *carabaos*, object of Prep = *of*
predeterminer, └───┘ determiners = *the* and *fifty* (part of the prepositional phrase Adj =

SPron, plural = <u>few</u>   *of the fifty carabaos,* modifying plural SPron = <u>few</u>)

○ 4) *Adjective as subject of the sentence,* when the noun is not necessary to stress the obvious.

◊ The <u>poor</u> \ **are** patient people.   (The poor <u>people</u> \ **are** patient.)

↑
SN, plural (Adj) = <u>poor</u>, *adjective* in the phrase = *poor* <u>people</u>

◊ The <u>wounded</u> / **were treated** by doctors.

↑

SN, plural = <u>wounded</u> (Adj), past participle of AV = **wound**) in the phrase = *wounded* <u>men</u>

◊ (Note: To: All Concerned., in official memo greeting, *concerned* is the past participle of the verb *concern* used as a noun ; [Adj, as in the phrase *concerned teachers*])

□ Determiner and Predeterminer in a Noun Phrase

• The *determiner* is an *adjective* which signals that a *noun* is coming; it is also called a *noun marker* or *marker*. The four kinds of determiners are 1) *articles*, 2) *pointing* or *demonstrative pronouns*, 3) *possessive pronouns* and 4) *numbers*. A determiner functions as *adjective* in the sentence.

○ 1) *Articles* = *a, an* and *the*

◊ *A* <u>hen</u> / **laid** two-dozen eggs.   (indefinite article =*a*a)

◊ *An* <u>orange</u> / **dropped** from the tree.   (indefinite article = a*n*)

◊ *The* bougainvilleas **/ were planted** last year. definite article = *the*)
o 2) *Pointing Pronouns or Demonstratives* = *this, these, that* and *those*
◊ *This* book \ **is** our reference.   (singular = *this)*
◊ *These* trees **/ were knocked** down during the storm.(plural = *these)*
◊ *That* girl \ **is** Junjie's friend.   (singular = *that)*
◊ *Those* cars **/ arrived** yesterday from Malaysia.   (plural = *those)*
o 3) *Possessives* = *her, hers, his, my, mine, our, ours, your, yours, their, theirs,* and *its*
◊ *Her* racquet **/ was broken** during practice.   (*her)*
◊ *The* gift brought by Cielo \ **is** *hers* and not *mine*.   (*hers, mine)*
◊ *Our* program **/ did not push** through because of the rain.   (our)
o 4) *Numbers* = *three, few, many, some, a hundred, ten thousand* . . . etc.
◊ *Three* coins **/ were dropped** in the fountain.
◊ *Many* men **/ are called** but *few* volunteers **/ are chosen.**
• Determiners and Predeterminers – The *determiner* is an *adjective* serving as a *noun marker giving signal that a noun is coming.* The *predeterminer* is a *pronoun,* like *many, some, several,* etc., serving as the *simple subject* of the sentence and the verb agrees with it.

  ◊ Many *of the forty students* \ **were** absent.

                ↑   ↑ ↑   N = *students*, object of Prep = *of*
  predeterminer,   └──┘ determiners (the, forty)

  (SPron, plural) = many [complete subject noun phrase or SPron, plural] = Many *of the forty students* ; predeterminer serving as the subject of the sentence = many ; prepositional phrase = *of the forty students* as Adj modifying many ; linking verb [LV] agreeing with many = **were**)

◊ Several *of our five flashlights* **/ need** new batteries.

                ↑   ↑ ↑   N = *flashlights*, object of Prep = *of*
  predeterminer,   └──┘   determiners our, five

  (SPron, plural) = Several, [predeterminer used as subject of the sentence] ; prepositional phrase

Adj, modifying <u>several</u> = *of our five flashlights* ; possessive Pron as Adj modifying *flashlight* = *our* ; action verb [AV], agreeing with <u>Several</u> = **need**)

□ Verb or Verb Phrase and Its Forms as Predicate of the Sentence

• Verbs are grouped into three: 1) the *Action* Verbs, 2) the *State of Being* Verbs or *Linking* Verbs and 3) the *Auxiliary* or *Helping* Verbs.

• 1. Action Verbs – The **action verb** (**AV**) indicates or describes the *action* or *movement of someone* or *something* or *what someone or something* **does** or **did**. An *action* may be either *physical* or *mental*. A *physical movement* can be *observed*, while a *mental action* or *process cannot be seen*.

◊ *Physical* action verb (AV) = The <u>surgeon</u> / **operated** on the patient for three hours.

                                                                            ↑

AV (physical action; *what someone did*) =`` **operated**

◊ *Mental* action verb (AV) = <u>Mother</u> / **believe**s that breast milk is good for her baby   ↑

AV (mental action; *what someone thinks*) = **believes**

o 2) Some *action* verbs may be both *physical* or *mental*.

    ◊ *Physical* and *mental* = <u>Rino</u> / **writes** his wartime memoirs.
                                      ↑
    AV (physical and mental actions) = **writes**

□ Exercise 11 : Jot down each *action verb* and indicate whether it is *physical* or *mental action*.

1. Eden's guest arrived late and stumbled on the sleeping cat.

2. Regulo hoped he would win in the lottery.

3. Nature has a way of striking back at those who indiscriminately cut trees.

4. Everyone thought it was good for the people to continue the irrigation project.

5. Some politicians want to postpone the barangay elections.

6. The peace talk in Mindanao suffered a setback anew with the death of a Catholic bishop.

7. Orlando said that globalization was bad for the sugar industry.

8. A landslide occurred when the rain came. .

9. The school won first place in the War on Waste (WOW) contest in the provincial level.

10. I enjoy movies, but I seldom go to a movie house.

o Action verbs may consist of several words in the form of *auxiliaries* or *helping* verbs (HV) and *main* verbs (MV), resulting in action verb (AV) phrases (HV + MV).

◊ Nature / **is punishing** the wantonly destructive people with storms and flash floods.
↑   ↑

AV, present participle as MV = **punishing** (base form = *punish*)

HV = **is** (base form = *be*)

(AV phrase [**HV + MV**] = **is punishing**)

• 2. Linking Verbs – The **linking verb** expresses the *condition* or *state of existence* of *someone* or *something* and is also called **state of being verb** (**SOBV**). *Be* verbs or verbs *to be* are used as *linking verbs*.

o *Be* verbs **am, is, are, was** and **were** as *linking verbs* (**LV**) *connect* the *complements* or *completers* to the *subjects* of the sentences. *Complements* or *completers identify* or *describe* the *subject nouns* or *subject pronouns* of the *sentences*.

◊ *Linking* verb = The hero \ **is** dead.   (*linking verb* [LV] or *state of being verb* (SOBV) = **is**)

◊ Chris \ **was** the *engineer* who designed the bridge.
↑   ↑

SN LV, past time = **was** (SOBV = *be*), linking complement = *engineer* to SN = Chris

o The *linking verb* (LV) **am** (SOBV = *be*) is *used in only one situation* -- connecting or linking the complement or completer (instructor) to the subject pronoun I.

◊ I \ **am** an *instructor.*

SPron = I̲ LV, present time = **am** (SOBV = *be*), linking complement = *instructor* to SPron = I̲

○ *Be* verb as *helping verb* in a verb phrase followed by a prepositional phrase.

◊ I̲ / **am disappointed** by her comments.

SPron = I̲ | MV, --ed form, past participle = **disappointed** (V base form = *disappoint*)

HV, present = **am** (V special form = *be*) [**am** is used only with pronoun I̲]

>AV phrase, *present time, passive voice* (**HV** + **MV**) = **am disappointed**

○Deleting the prepositional phrase *by her comments* makes **am** a *linking verb*, connecting *disappointed* (*past participle*), a predicate adjective (PA) complement to the subject pronoun I̲.

◊ I̲ \ **am** *disappointed.*

(LV = **am**, connects predicate adjective [PA] =

LV   *disappointed* to SPron = I̲)

○ An action verb that can be replaced in a sentence by a *be verb* is a *linking verb*. **Slam** is a linking verb as in *The door* **slammed** *shut.* = The door **is** shut. **Drop** is also a linking verb as in *He* **dropped** *dead.* = He **is** dead.

◊ The guava \ **tastes** sour.   ◊ The guava \ **is** sour.

SN, singular AV, --s form, present LV, present time = **is** (SOBV = *be*), time = **tastes** (V base form = *taste*), agreeing with singular SN = guava agreeing with singular SN = guava

Some action verbs that are also linking verbs:

Act	become	feel	grow	look	remain	seem	sound	taste
appear	drop	get	keep	prove	run	slam	stay	turn

◊ <u>Rizal Day</u> \ **will be** on Sunday this year. ◊ <u>Rizal Day</u> \ **is** on Sunday this year.

                LV   (AV phrase = **will be** can be replaced by **is**)

       ◊ <u>It</u> \ **shall have been** a great achievement to win her love.
◊ <u>It</u> \ **is** a great achievement.

LV   (AV phrase = **shall have been** can be replaced by **is**)

◊ <u>It</u> \ **could have been** a tame lion that he plays with.
◊ <u>It</u> \ **is** a tame lion.

 SPron, singular   LV (AV phrase = **could have been** can be replaced by LV = **is**)

○ Some linking verbs are forms of the verb *be* and *modals* that are in phrases:

can be	could be	have been	as been	had been	could have been	shall have been	should have been
shall be	should be	will have been	would have been	will be	would be	may have been	might have been
may be	might be	must be	must have been	ought to have been			

☐ Exercise 12 : Write on your paper the *linking verbs*.

1. Lions can be gentle at times.

2. Ann's doughnut tasted too sweet.

3. Sandra, who has a car, is a teacher.

4. A boy appears nosy to the consternation of the old lady.

5. Fatima became a nurse.

6. Inocencio would have been an engineer by now.

7. Norma gets beautiful every day.

8. Is the paint dry?

9. The audience fell silent.

10. Olive has been adamant for days.

☐ Exercise 13 : List down all the *action* or *linking verbs* found in the following paragraphs.

Arthritic patients suffer more pain during the cold months of January and February, because of the change in the barometric pressure in the afflicted joints. Arthritis or rayuma is one of the immunologic diseases.

What are immunologic diseases? These are allergies, immune-deficiency, reproductive immunologic condition and auto-immune disorders.

Autoimmunity occurs when the immune system is hyper-responsive and produces antibodies that attack a person's own body with symptoms varying on the kind of disorder and the part of the body affected. This could be in the form of multi-organ involvement, like lupus that is characterized by the inflammation on vital organs like the skin, lungs, heart, brain liver and kidneys. Although the exact cause of lupus is unknown, a combination of genetic and environmental factors such as viruses has been implicated.

Symptoms of the disease commonly include fatigue, weight loss, falling hair, photosensitive rash, recurrent oral or nasal ulcers, joint pain and swelling.

• 3.The Auxiliary or Helping Verbs Used in Verb Phrases – The **auxiliary** or **helping verbs** (**HV**) that work hand in hand with the participle forms of the action verbs as main verbs (**MV**) and constitute the action verb (AV) phrases (**HV + MV**) are 1) *be verbs* **am, is, are,** was and were, 2) *modals* can, could, may, might, must, shall, should, will, would and ought, 3) action verbs do, does and did, and 4) action verbs have, has and had.

- 1) The *Be Verbs* as Helping Verbs in the Action Verb Phrases

  ○ (1) The *present time* AV phrase, *expressing action now taking place* (**HV** + **MV**) = **is enrolled / are enrolled**; HV, present time = **is** (for singular subject) **/ are** (for plural subject); MV, --**ed** form, past participle = **enrolled**

  ◊ We **/ are enrolled** in medical technology.
  SPron, ↑   ↑   ↑ MV, --**ed** form, *past participle* = **enrolled** (V base form = *enroll*)

  plural   HV, present time = **are** (HV = *be*), agreeing with plural SPron = we

  ○ (2) The *past time* AV phrase, *action completed* (**HV** + **MV**) = **was marooned / were marooned**, HV, past time = **was** (for singular subject) **/ were** (for plural subject); MV, --**ed** form, *past participle* = **marooned**

  ◊ The cow **/ was marooned** by the snowstorm in the forest.
  SN, singular ↑   ↑   ↑

  MV, --**ed** form, *past participle* = **marooned** (V base form = *maroon*)

  HV, past time = **was** (HV = *be*), agreeing with singular SN = cow

  ○ (3) The *present progressive time* AV phrase, *action started and continuing at the time of speaking* (**HV** + **MV**) = **is dancing / are dancing**; HV, present time = **is** (for singular subject) **/ are** (for plural subject); MV, --**ing** form, *present participle* = **dancing**

  The boys **/ are dancing** the hula.
  SN, plural ↑   ↑   ↑

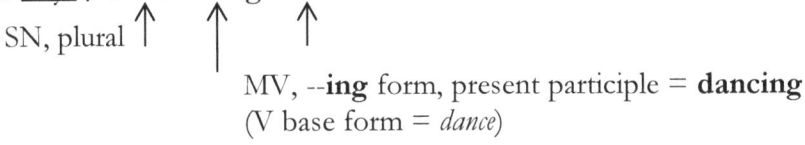

  MV, --**ing** form, present participle = **dancing** (V base form = *dance*)

HV, present time = **are** (HV = *be*), agreeing with plural SN = boys

o (4) The *past progressive time* AV phrase, *action was started and going on prior to another event* (**HV + MV**) = **was building / were building**; HV, past time = **was** (for singular subject) **/ were** (for plural subject); MV, –**ing** verb form or *present participle* = **building**

◊ Julius **/ was building** a birdhouse when his guests came.
SN,

MV, --**ing** form, *present participle* = **building** (V base form = *build*)

singular HV, past time = **was** (HV *be*), agreeing with singular SN = Jun

• 2) *Modals* as Helping Verbs in Verb Phrases Showing Present and Future Actions

o The *modals* (Symbol = **HVM**) **can, will, shall, may, must** and **ought** (present forms) and **could, would, should** and **might** (past forms) may indicate *futurity* or show also *generally accepted ideas*. **Ought**, a *special helping* verb, is followed by an infinitive. Modals as helping verbs express: 1) *ability* = **can wash**, 2) *simple future time* = **will wash**, 3) *obligation* = **shall wash**, 4) *probability (moral obligation)* = **should wash**, 5) *necessity* and *probability* = **must wash**, 6) *possibility* = **may** or **might wash**, and 7) *obligation* or *strong likelihood* = **ought to wash**.

o (1) The *simple present* and *future time* **AV** phrase (**HVM + MV**) = **can paint**, showing *ability to do things* or *generally accepted idea*

◊ Novie **/ can paint** landscapes.   (Simple present time = Novie **/ paints** landscapes.)

SN,   MV, **base** form, present time = **paint**
singular   HVM = **can** (HV modal, present form)

o(1a) The *simple past time* **AV** phrase (**HVM + MV**) = **could sing**, showing *generally accepted idea* or *ability to do things in the past that may continue at present and in the future*

◊ Emma **/ could sing** liltingly as a little girl.

SN,↑

          MV, **base** form, present time = **sing**

          singulat   HVM, past form = **could**
          (HV modal, present form = *can*)

○ (2) The *simple future time* **AV** phrase (**HVM** + **MV**) = **will address**, showing *future action*

◊ An <u>alumnus</u> / **will address** this year's graduates.
          ↑   ↑ ↑
    SN,

          MV, **base** form, present time = **address**

          singular   HVM, present form = **will**
          (HV modal, present form)

○ (2a) The *simple future time* **AV** phrase (**HVM** + **MV**) = **will vote**, showing *future action with determination* (when used with SPron = <u>I</u>, first person)

◊ <u>I</u> / **will vote** in the coming elections for the national officials.

   SPron,↑   ↑ ↑MV, **base** form, present time = **vote**

     singular   HVM, present form = **will** (HV modal, present form)

○ (3) The *simple future time* **AV** phrase (**HVM** + **MV**) = **would listen**, showing *future habitual action*

◊ The <u>men</u> / **would listen** to the commander's speech during programs.
                   ↑
    SN, plural ↑   ↑

          MV, **base** form, present time = **listen**

          HVM, past form = **would** (HV modal, present form = *will*)

○ (3a) The *simple future time* **AV** phrase (**HVM** + **MV**) = **shall wash**, indicating *future obligation*

◊ <u>Tony</u> / **shall wash** the car.
                 ↑
      SN,↑   ↑   MV, **base** form, present time = **wash**

48   A Guide in the Study of the Usage of the American English

        singular   HVM = **shall** (HV modal, present form)

o (3b) *The simple future time* **AV** phrase (**HVM + MV**) = **shall invite**, indicating *simple future action*

◊ We / **shall invite** you to the conference as observer.
    ↑   ↑   ↑
  SPron,   MV, **base** form, present time = **invite**

   plural   HVM = **shall** (HV modal, present form)

o (4) *The simple future time* **AV** phrase (**HVM + MV**) = **should clean**, showing *future obligation*

◊ They / **should clean** their rooms.
    ↑   ↑   ↑
  SPron, plural   MV, **base** form, present time = **clean**

             HVM, past form = **should** (HV modal, present form = shall)

o (4a) *The simple future time* **AV** phrase (**HVM + MV**) = **should welcome**, showing *moral obligation*

◊ We / **should welcome** all visitors to our country.
    ↑   ↑   ↑
  SPron,   MV, **base** form, present time = **welcome**

  plural   HVM, past form = **should** (HV modal, present form = *shall*)

o (5) *The simple future time* **AV** phrase (**HVM + MV**) = **might work**, showing *possibility of future action*

◊ Regie / **might work** as a lifeguard.
    ↑   ↑   ↑
  SN,↑   MV, **base** form, present time = **work**

    singular   HVM, past form = **might** (HV modal, present form = *may*)

o (6) *The simple future time* **AV** phrase (**HVM + MV**) = **must come**, showing *necessity; lawful obligation or duty to do ; probability or likelihood of some act to be done*

   ◊ They / **must come** to the office immediately or they shall lose their jobs.
          ↑   ↑   ↑

SPron,   MV, **base** form, present time = **come**

plural   HVM, future form =**must** (HV modal)

◊ <u>Serge</u> / **must become** a doctor to inherit his grandfather's medical center estate.

SN,↑   ↑   ↑ MV, **base** form, present time = **become**

singular   HVM, future form = **must** (HV modal)

○ (7) *The present time AV phrase* (**HVM + MV**) = **ought** *to win*, expressing *necessity, strong likelihood, or expedience,* (HVM = **ought**, followed by *to* & **verb** as MV, infinitive phrase, **base** form = *to win*)

◊ <u>We</u> / **ought to win** medals in the Olympics.

SPron,↑   ↑   ↑MV, infinitive phrase= **to win**

plural   HVM, present time = **ought** (HV modal)

◊ The <u>guard</u> / **ought *not* to allow** anyone in the compound.

SN, ↑   ↑   ↑MV, infinitive = **to allow**

singular   HVM, future time = **ought** (HV = modal)

Adv = *not, essential* part of the verb phrase = **ought *not* to allow**

◊ The <u>drainage</u> / **ought to be cleared** of garbage as a measure of minimizing flood.

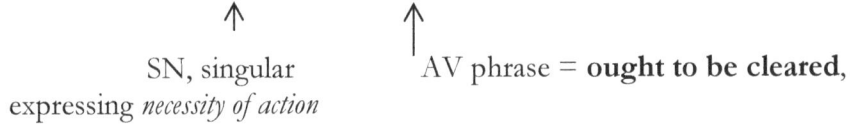

↑   ↑

SN, singular   AV phrase = **ought to be cleared**, expressing *necessity of action*

• Clarification on the Use of **Shall, Will, Should** and **Would**

○1) *Simple futurity* or simple future time = **shall** is used in the *first person* or with first person pronouns <u>I</u> and <u>we</u>, **will**, in the *second person* or with second person pronoun <u>you</u> and in the *third person* or with third person pronouns <u>he</u>, <u>she</u>, <u>it</u>, and <u>they</u>

◊ <u>I</u> / **shall vote** in the coming elections for the national officials. (<u>I</u> = *first person*)

◊ We / shall invite you to the conference as observer. (We = *first person*)

◊ You / will need tents in the research work. (You = *second person*)

◊ He / will meet Jim at the mall.
(He = *third person*)

◊ They / will undergo training in special warfare.
(They = *third person*)

○2) *Determination, compulsion, threat, obligation* or *promise* (willingness to do something) = **will** is used in the *first person* or with first person pronouns I and we and **shall** in the *second person* or second person pronoun *you* and *third person* or with third person pronouns he or she and they

◊ We / will invite his parents to the awarding rites.
(We = *first person*)

◊ You / shall ask permission from the landowner.
(You = *second person*)

◊ He / shall see to it that the rules are observed.
(He = *third person*)

◊ They / shall follow the program of instruction strictly.
(They = *third person*)

○3) *Moral obligation, necessity, probability, future or past condition* = **should** (Pronouns in all three persons)

◊ I / should vote in the elections as a citizen in our country.

◊ We / should register in order to vote.

◊ You / should assist your younger sibling.

◊ She / should present proof of birth to qualify as scholar.

◊ They / should pay the mortgage liens on the lot.

○(3a) **should** = probability, futurity with implication of doubt, future or past condition

◊ *probability* = The sea / should be choppy if it rains this afternoon.

◊ *futurity, with doubt* = <u>They</u> **/ should come** as a grateful gesture.

◊ *future* or *past condition* = <u>She</u> **/ should have been elected** had she campaigned earnestly.

○ 4) *Habitual* or *customary action* = **would** (in all three persons)

○ (4) **would** = <u>habitual</u> or <u>customary</u> <u>action</u> (Pronouns in all three persons)

◊ <u>I</u> **/ would feed** the pigs until they are ready for the market.

◊ <u>We</u> **/ would watch** the sun go down and enjoy nature's beauty.

◊ <u>You</u> **/ would enjoy** fishing in the lake there.

◊ <u>She</u> **/ would sew** kid dresses to sell every weekend.

◊ <u>They</u> **/ would swim** in the river for hours.

- 3) The Verb **Do** as Action (**AV**) and as Helping Verb (**HV**)

○ **Do**, a transitive action verb, along with its other forms, **does** and **did**, is used also as *helping verb* in a verb phrase in the (1) *interrogative*, (2) *emphatic*, or (3) *urgent imperative sentence* constructions. The main verb in the verb phrase using **do** as helping verb is *always* in the *base form* or **do**. Interrogative sentences use verb phrases, *present time* = **do** + (subject) + **do**, for <u>plural</u> subject; *present* time, **does** + (subject) + **do**, for <u>singular</u> subject and *past time*, **did** + (subject) + **do**, for <u>plural</u> or <u>singular</u> subject

○ (1a) Statement using **AV**, **base** form, simple present time = **do**, agreeing with <u>plural</u> subject

◊ The <u>girls</u> **/ do** their cooking at the canteen.   (*Statement*)
  SN, plural ↑   ↑   O

AV, **base** form, simple present time = **do**, agreeing with plural SN = <u>girls</u>

○ (1b) Interrogative (Transformation of statement to question) using **HV**, **base** form, simple present time = **do**, agreeing with <u>plural</u> subject in an interrogative action verb (AV) phrase. The main verb (MV) is always in the base form in interrogative sentences.

◊ **Do** the <u>girls</u> **/ do** their cooking at the canteen?   (*Question*)
     ↑   ↑   ↑

SN   MV, **base** form, present time = **do** plural

HV, present time = **do**, agreeing with plural SN = girls

>AV phrase (interrogative), *present time* (**HV** + **MV**) = **do** + (girls) + **do**

○ (1c) Statement using **AV**, **--s** form, simple present time = **does**, agreeing with singular subject

◊ Trixia / **does** her chores gladly.   (*Statement*)
   ↑   ↑   ○

SN, singular   AV, irregular, **--s** form, simple present time = **does** (V base form = *do*), agreeing with singular SN = Trixia

○ (1d) Interrogative (Transformation of statement to question) using **HV, --s** form, simple present time = **does**, agreeing with singular subject in an interrogative AV phrase

◊ **Does** Trixia **do** her chores gladly?   (*Question*)
  ↑   ↑SN ↑   ↑   ↑○

MV, irregular, **base** form, present time = **do**

HV, present time = **does** (V base form = *do*), agreeing with singular SN =Trixia

>AV phrase (interrogative), *present time* (**HV** + **MV**) = **does** + (Trixia) + **do**

○ (1e) Statement using **AV**, **--ed** form, simple past time = **did**, for plural or singular subject

◊ The men / **did** their masonry well.   (*Statement*)
         ↑   ↑AV, irregular, **--ed** form, simple past time = **did** (V base form = do)

SN, plural

○ (1c) Interrogative (Transformation of statement to question) using **HV, --ed** form, simple past time, **did,** for plural or singular subject in a verb phrase

◊ **Did** the men / **do** their masonry well?   (*Question*)
    ↑

SN ↑ ↑ MV, **base** form, present time = **do**

HV, past time = **did** (V base form = *do*), indicating past action

>AV phrase (interrogative), past time (**HV + MV**) = **did** + (men) + **do**

○ (2a) Statement using **AV** = **-s** form, simple present time = **loves**, agreeing with <u>singular</u> subject

◊ <u>Leilani</u> **/ loves** her country very much.   (*Statement*)
   ↑   ↑

SN,

   singular   AV, **-s** form, present time = **loves** (V base form = *love*), agreeing with

singular SN = Leilani

○ (2b) Statement using **AV** = **base** form, simple present time = **like**, agreeing with <u>plural</u> subject

◊ <u>They</u> **/ like** prawns very much.   (*Statement*)
   ↑   ↑
SPron,

   singular   AV, **base** form, simple present time = **like**, agreeing with <u>plural</u> SPron = <u>they</u>

○ (2c) Emphatic statement using **HV**, simple present time = **does**, agreeing with <u>singular</u> subject in a verb phrase = **does + love**

◊ <u>Lee</u> **/ does love** his country so that he joined the Army. (*Emphatic present*)
   ↑   ↑   ↑

MV, regular, **base** form, present time = **love**

SPron,   V, present time = **does** (V base form = *do*), agreeing with singular SN = Lee

>AV phrase *(emphatic), present time,* (**HV + MV**) = **does + love**

○(2d) Emphatic statement using **HV**, **base** form, simple present time = **do**, agreeing with <u>plural</u> subject

◊ They / do like prawns very much.(*Emphatic present*)
SPron, plural ↑ ↑ ↑MV, base form, present time = like

HV, present time = do (V base form), agreeing with plural SPron = they

>AV phrase (emphatic), *present time* (HV + MV) = do + like

○ (2e) Emphatic statement using HV, past time = did, agreeing with plural or singular subject

◊ Herman / *did* sing ballads at the dance hall.   (*Emphatic past*)
N, singular ↑   ↑ ↑MV, base form, present time = sing

HV, past time = did (V base form = *do*)

>AV phrase (emphatic), *past time* HV + MV) = did + sing

● (3a) Imperative statement using HV in its base form = do, agreeing with the only subject pronoun you, in the *plural sense* (you, referring to one or more persons, omitted in actual usage)

○ (3a) *Plain imperative* = S, plural pronoun = (You) / AV, base form, present time = stop

◊ (You) / Stop singing now. (Stop singing now.) (*Imperative*)

↑AV, base form, present time = stop

○ (3b) Urgent imperative statement using HV, simple present time = do, agreeing with subject Pron (You), omitted in actual usage in *present time* AV phrase

◊ (You) / *Do* stop singing now. (Do stop singing now.)   (*Urgent imperative*)   ↑

HV,   ↑MV, base form, present time = stop

present time = do (V base form = *do*), agreeing with SPron = (you)

>AV phrase (urgent imperative), *present time*, (HV + MV) = *do* stop

●4) The Verb Have as Action Verb (AV) and as Helping Verb (HV)

○ Have as AV may replace take; infinitive to have has the same meaning as to take.

o The *simple present time* AV, **base** form, *active voice* = **have**, for plural subject ╱ (**has**, for singular subject), *indicating action being* taken *by the students*

◊ The students ╱ have an educational trip.
　　SN, plural　　　AV, **base** form, simple present time, active voice = **have**, agreeing with plural SN = students

o) The *present perfect time* **AV** phrase = *showing action that had just been completed at the time of speaking and reflecting an emphatic situation*, active voice (**HV + MV**) = **have had**, for plural subject ╱ (**has had**, for singular subject) ; HV, *present time*, base form = *have* ; MV, **--en** form = **had**

◊ The seniors ╱ have had their meeting at the auditorium.
　　SN, plural　　　　　MV, **--en** form, past participle = **had**
(V base form = *have*)

　　HV, present time, V base form, agreeing with plural SN = seniors
>AV phrase, *present perfect time, active voice* (**HV + MV**) = **have had**

• 4a) **Have** as Helping Verb (**HV**) Used in Sentence Transformation

o **Have** functions also as helping verb in the 1) *interrogative* sentence constructions and 2) with a *modal* and a *be verb,* may also serve as part of *linking verb phrases.*

o (1)Transformation of the *simple past time statement* to a *question,* using **have** as helping verb

◊ The students ╱ wrote their parents about their educational trip. (*S*
　　SN, plural　　　AV, irregular, **--ed** form, simple past time= **wrote** (V base form = *write*)

o (1a) The *interrogative present perfect time* **AV** phrase, plural subject (**HV + MV**) = **have written** ; the subject SN = students, placed between helping (HV) and main verb (MV)

◊ **Have** the students **written** their parents about their educational trip? (*Question*)

SN, plural　　　　　MV, --**en** form, past participle =
written (V base form = *write*)　　HV, present time = **have** (V base
form = *have*), agreeing with plural SN = students

> *interrogative* AV phrase, *present perfect time* (**HV** + [SN] + **MV**) = **have**
+ (students) + **written**

○(1b) The *interrogative present perfect time* **AV** phrase, singular subject (**HV**
+ **MV**) = **has endorsed**; the singular SN = principal placed between
the HV and MV

◊ **Has** the principal **endorsed** the educational trip to the
superintendent for approval?

　　　↑　　　　↑

　　　　　　　　　　　　　↑ MV, --**ed** form, past participle =
endorsed (V base form = *endorse*)　　SN, singular

　　　HV, present time = **has** (V base form = *have*), agreeing with
singular SN = principal

> *interrogative* AV phrase, *present perfect time* (**HV** + [SN] + **MV**) = **has**
+ (principal) + **endorsed**

○ The *past perfect time* **AV** phrase, singular or plural subject (**HV** + **MV**)
= **had written**

◊ The students / **had written** their parents about their educational
trip.　　(*Statement*)

SN, plural　　↑　　　↑ MV, --**en** form, past participle = **written**
(V base form = *write*)　　　HV, past time = **had** (V
base form = *have*)

>AV phrase, *past perfect time* (**HV** + **MV**) = **had written**

○ 1c) *Question in direct response to a statement in the past perfect time AV phrase*
; question uses HV **had**, as the action in the statement was made in the
past

◊ **Had** the students **written** their parents about their educational trip?
(*Question*)　↑　　↑　　　↑

　　　　　　　SN, plural　　MV, --**en** form, past participle=
written (V base form = *write*)

HV, past time = **had** (V base form = *have*)

> *interrogative* AV phrase, *past perfect time,* **HV** + [SN] + **MV**) = **had** + (students) + **written**

○ 2a) **Have** in a linking verb phrase (*modal* + HV *be*) = **could have been**

◊ It \ **could have been** a stormy day in the islands that Silvino was forced to stay home.

SPron, It   HVM, LV phrase, past time =**could have been**; equivalent = **was** (HV = *be*)

○ 2b) **Could have been** as linking verb phrase replaced by **was** (SOBV = *be*)

◊ It \ **was** a stormy day in the islands that Silvino was forced to stay home.

LV, past time (verb *be*) = **was**

SPron

- 4) **Have** Is the Helping Verb (**HV**) Used in the Perfect Time AV Phrase

○ (1) The *present perfect time* AV phrase = *action that had just been completed at the time,* (**HV** + **MV**) = **have patrolled**, for plural subject / (**has patrolled**, for singular subject) ; HV, present time = **have** ; MV, regular, --**ed** form or past participle = **patrolled**

◊ The soldiers / **have patrolled** the area for months.

SN, plural   MV, --**ed** form, past participle = **patrolled** (V base form = *patrol*)

HV, **base** form, present time = **have**, agreeing with plural SN = soldiers

○(1a) The *present perfect time* AV phrase = *action that had just been completed at the time,* (**HV** + **MV**) = **has lent**, for singular subject / (**have lent**, for plural subject) ; HV, *present time* = **has** ; MV, irregular, --**en** form or past participle = **lent**

◊ <u>Phil</u> / **has lent** his car to Ken.
   SN,↑   ↑   ↑MV, --**en** form, past participle = **lent** (V base form = *lend*)

   singular   HV, present time = **has** (V base form = *have*), agreeing with singular SN = <u>Phil</u>

○ (2) The *past perfect time* **AV** phrase =*action completed at the time of speaking*, (**HV** + **MV**) = **had given**, for <u>plural</u> or <u>singular</u> subject ; HV, *past time* = **had** ; MV, irregular, --**en** form = **given**

◊ <u>They</u> / **had given** a tidy sum of money to Ren.
   SPron,↑   ↑   ↑ MV, --**en** form, past participle= **given** (V base form = give)

   plural   HV, past time = **had**   (V base form = *have*)

○ (3) The *future perfect time* **AV** phrase = *action completed at a future time*, HVM, *present form* = **will**, (**HVM** + **HV**, + **MV**) = **will have married**, for <u>plural</u> or <u>singular</u> subject ; HV, present time = **have** ; MV, regular, --**ed** form = **married**

◊ <u>Ramy</u> / **will have married** Rolinda at this time.
   SN ,↑   ↑   ↑MV, -**ed** form, past participle = **married** (V base form = *marry*)

   singular   HV, present time = **have** (V base form = *have*)

   HVM, present time = **will** (V, *modal,* present form)

○ (4) The *present perfect progressive time* **AV** phrase = *action probably being done at the time*, (**HV** + **MHV** + **MV**) = **have been chatting**, for <u>plural</u> subject ∕ (**has been chatting**, for <u>singular</u> subject) ; HV, *present time* = **have** ; MHV, --**en** form = **been** ; MV, regular, --**ing** form = **chatting**

◊ The <u>girls</u> / **have been chatting** about the recent elopement of mutual friends.↑   ↑   ↑   ↑

   SN, plural

            MV, --**ing** form, present participle = **chatting** (V base form = *chat*)

            MHV, --**en** form = **been** (V base form = *be*)

HV, present time = **have** (V base form), agreeing with plural SN = girls

○ (4a) The *present perfect progressive time* **AV** phrase = *action probably being done at the time*, (**HV + MHV + MV**) = **has been calling**, for singular subject / (**have been calling**, for plural subject) ; HV, *present time* = **has** ; MHV, **--en** form = **been**, MV, regular, **--ing** form = **calling**

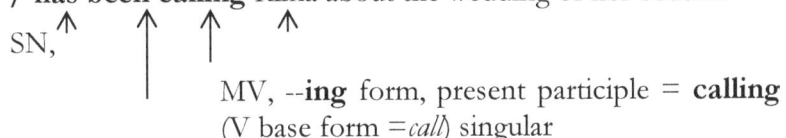

◊ Fe / **has been calling** Rima about the wedding of her cousin.
SN,↑　↑　↑　↑

　　　MV, **--ing** form, present participle = **calling**
　　　(V base form =*call*) singular

MHV, **--en** form = **been** (HV base form = *be*)

　　　HV, present time = **has** (V base form =*have*), agreeing with singular SN = Fe

○ (5) The *past perfect progressive time* AV phrase = *probability of one doing his job at an indicated past time*, (**HV + MHV + MV**) = **had been singing**, for plural or singular subject ; HV, *past time* = **had** ; MHV, **--en** form = **been** ; MV, regular, **--ing** form = **singing**

◊ Thelma / **had been singing** the whole day yesterday.
SN,↑　↑　↑　↑

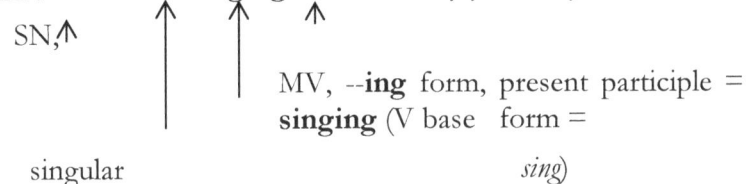

　　　MV, **--ing** form, present participle = **singing** (V base form =

singular　　　　　　　　　　　*sing*)

　　　MHV, past participle = **been** (HV base form = *be*)

　　　HV, past time = **had** (V base form = *have*)

○ (6) The *future perfect progressive time* **AV** phrase = *a condition of one being under obligation ought to be doing his job*, (**HVM + HV + MHV + MV**) = **will have been cleaning**, for plural or singular subject ; HVM, *present time* = **will** ; HV, present time = **have** ; MHV, **--en** form = **been** ; MV, regular, **--ing** form = **cleaning**

◊ Rea / **will have been cleaning** her employer's house at the end of December.↑　↑　↑　↑　↑

SN, MV, --ing form, present participle
= **cleaning** (V base form singular = *clean*)

MHV, past participle = **been** (HV base form = *be*)

HV, present = **have** (V base form = *have*)

HVM, present time = **will** (V, modal)

☐ Exercise 14 : Copy each *perfect time verb phrase* and indicate the *time* of each.

The explosion had been caused by a bomb, the initial report said. But the police investigators had not issued any statement out of speculation. The head of the fact-finding investigators had been entertaining a theory that it was gas explosion. The crack on the hillside where the blast had occurred was about five kilometers from an active volcano. The volcanologists had debunked the idea; their seismic equipment did not register any activity that may have come from underground.

Meanwhile, the bickering among the investigators would have sent wrong signals to the residents of the area. The mayor had promptly tagged the local rebels as the group behind the explosion. The rebel group had denied the accusation, but by then their exiled leader would have relished the confusion that might cause the local residents to lose faith in the capability of the government machinery to protect them from harm.

☐ Verb Tense

• Verb tense, being the most complex and controversial grammatical category, makes grammarians disagree on the way of analyzing the linguistic markers of time relations.

• The verb (V) is the only part of speech that can show a *change in time or tense by a change in the verb form itself.* Every verb phrase includes a *verb* and its *tense. Tense or time is the property of verbs showing differences in time or condition.*

• Grammarians differ as to how many tenses an English verb can have. Traditional grammarians say that the English finite verb has *six tenses.*

Tense	Singular Subject	Plural Subject

1) the simple present -- <u>He</u> / **walks**.   -- <u>They</u> / walk.
2) the simple past   -- <u>He</u> / **walked**.   -- <u>They</u> / **walked**.
3) the simple future -- <u>He</u> / **will walk**. -- <u>They</u> / **will** walk.
4).the present perfec -- <u>He</u> / **has walked**. -- <u>They</u> / **have** walked.
5) the past perfect (pluperfect) -- <u>He</u> / **had walked**.   -- <u>They</u> / **had walked**.
6) the future perfect -- <u>He</u> / **will have walked**. -- <u>They</u> / **will have walked**.

- Later, they add these two:

1) the progressive   -- <u>He</u> / **is walking**. – <u>They</u> / **are walking**
2) the emphatic   -- <u>He</u> / **does walk**. – <u>They</u> / **do walk**.
                      -- <u>He</u> / **did walk**.   – <u>They</u> / **did walk**.

`• Some grammarians say there are *fifteen tenses*; others, *twenty-four* and a few, *seventy-five*. Most people, however, seem to agree on *twelve*.

1) the simple present -- <u>He /</u> **walks**.   -- <u>They</u> / **walk**.
2) the simple past   -- <u>He</u> / **walked**.   -- <u>They</u> / **walked**.
3) the simple future   -- <u>He</u> / **will walk**. -- <u>They</u> / **will walk**.
4) the present progressive -- <u>He</u> / **is wallking**. -- <u>They</u> / **are walking**.
5) the past progressive -- <u>He</u> / **was walking**. -- <u>They</u> /**were walking**.
6) the future progressive -- <u>He</u> / **will be walking**. -- <u>They</u> / **will be walking**.
7) the present perfect
   (continuing past) -- He / **has walked**.   – They / **have walked**.
8) the past perfect
   (completed past) -- <u>He</u> / **had walked**. – <u>They</u> / **had walked**.
9) the future perfect

(completed in the future) -- He / will have walked. --They / will have walked.

10) the present perfect
progressive   -- He / has been walking.
– They / have been walking.

11) the past perfect progressive   -- He / had been walking.– They / had been walking.

12) the future perfect progressive   -- He / will have been walking. – They / will have been walking.

o The action verb **walk** is both intransitive and transitive. It is used above in the intransitive form. The sentence pattern is Subject + Verb or S + V = He / walks. / They / walk. It is transitive if an object is added to the sentence = He / walks the beet farm. They / walk the talk. (Subject + Verb + Object or S + V + O) [Note: *walk the talk* is an idiom to put into fruition or process of development something thought of or planned or promised.]

• The modern approach to the study of tenses used in these notes is founded on the conventional twelve (12) tenses of the verb, in agreement with the traditional grammarians. However, one *gray area* on tense is the issue that *the English verb has six (6) original tenses, from which several other tenses are developed or derived*. The first three are the *simple tenses: 1) simple present, 2) simple past* and *3) simple future;* the other three are the *perfect tenses: 4) present perfect, 5) past perfect and 6) future perfect*. In the *simple tenses*, the adjective *simple connotes action* in *only one time frame*; the *perfect tenses* include the *idea of completion* at the *time of speaking, but may also indicate action that is continuing into the present.*

o Another *gray area* is that *the English verb has three principal parts*, referred to as its *basic forms,* which are 1) the **present tense**, 2) the **past tense** and 3) the **participles** (See Chart).

Actually, the *verb has **only two tenses** based on verb form.*

1) The **present tense** makes use of the **base** and **-s** or **-es** forms of the verb.

Ex. (a) regular verb, **base** form ending in vowel **e** = **receive** for plural subject

A. regular verb, **-s** form ending in vowel **e** = **receives** for singular subject

B. regular verb, **base** form in a consonant = **pack** for plural subject

C. regular verb, **-s** form ending in a consonant = **packs** for singular subject

D. irregular verb, **base** form ending in **o** = **go** for plural subject

E. irregular verb, **-es** form ending in **o** = **go<u>es</u>** for singular subject

F. irregular verb , **base** form ending in **ch** = **catch** for plural subject

G. irregular verb, **-es** form ending in **ch** = **catch<u>es</u>** for singular subject

2)   The *past tense* form of the regular verb gets the suffixes **-d** or **–ed.**

Ex. (a) regular verb, **base** form ending in vowel **e** = **receive** for plural subject;

(b) regular verb, **base** form ending in vowel **e** gets **-d** for its past tense = **receive<u>d</u>** for both plural and singular subjects

(c) regular verb **base** form ending in consonant has **-ed** added to it as past tense as in **pack** = **pack<u>ed</u>** for both plural and singular subjects

3)   There is *no basic verb form* for the **future tense.** The ***future tense*** may consist of the ***helping verb*** and ***main verb*** (*base form*) as in

Ex. (a) regular verb, **base** form = <u>I</u> / **shall return.** Or it may use the -s or -es) *form* and an <u>adverb</u> <u>of time,</u> as in = <u>He</u> / **returns** <u>tomorrow.</u>

(b) irregular verb, **base** form = **go,** as in <u>He</u> / **shall go** <u>this afternoon.</u> Or using the present form = <u>He</u> / **goes** this afternoon.

The other ***tenses*** are formed through *combinations* of the **participles** with *appropriate* **auxiliary** or **helping verbs** (*modals, be* verbs, and action verbs *do* and *have*). [See list of irregular verbs at the end of this compilation. Note that the terms *time* and *tense* are interchangeble. - Compiler]

oThe *simple present time*, the *simple past time* and the *simple future time* sentences are not hard to form. The other tenses using the participle to show *time* and *voice* make the study of the verb usage complicated. In the *active voice*, the chart shows that:

1) The **simple present time** of any English verb is the ***base form***, like **add** or **write**, which agrees in number with a *plural* subject; and 1a) the **–s or -es** form **adds** or **writes** for singular subject.

2) The **simple past time** is the **–ed form added** for the *regular verb with* plural or singular subject; the **simple past time** of the *irregular verb* **write** is **wrote** for plural or singular subject, which was arbitrarily assigned by grammarians.

3) The **simple future time** uses the modal **will** (**shall**) resulting in a phrase **will add** or **will write**; 3a) the **base** and the **–s forms (present tense)** of the action verb with an ***appropriate adverb of time*** are *also used* to ***show futurity***, thus, **add tomorrow** or **writes this Saturday**.

o The **present participle form** or **–ing form** is used as *main verb* of the *verb phrases* in the **progressive time**:

4) **present progressive time: is adding** or **are adding / is writing** or **are writing**

5) **past progressive time: was adding** or **were adding / was writing** or **were writing**

6) **future progressive time: will be adding / will be writing**

o The **perfect time** uses the **past participle** as main verb:

7) **present perfect time: has added** or **have added / has written** or **have written**

8) **past perfect time: had added / had written**

9) **future perfect time: will have added / will have written**

o The **perfect progressive time** makes use of the **present participle** for its *main verb*:

10) **present perfect progressive time: has been adding** or **have been adding / has been writing** or **have been writing**

11) **past perfect progressive time: had been adding / had been writing**

12) **future perfect progressive time: will have been adding / will have been writing**

• The **past participle forms,** with appropriate *helping* or *auxiliary verbs*, are used as *main verbs* of the verb phrases in the *passive voice*. The equivalent AV phrases of the 3 simple tenses: 1) the present time AV phrase = **is added** or **are added** / **is written** or **are written**, 2) the past time AV phrase = **was added** or **were added** / **was written** or **were written**, and 3) the future time AV phrase uses **modal** and **be** verb **will be added** / **will be written**. (The exercises below and in topic Clarification of the Twelve Times of the Verb show the forms of the AV phrases in the *passive voice*. Note that *only* sentences with *objects* or in the S + V + O sentence pattern can be changed to *passive*, because in the S + V sentence pattern, there is no *object* to become the *subject*.)

• Using the *Regular* Verb **Add** and the *Irregular* Verb **Write** in the *Active* and *Passive* Voices

1) The Simple Present Time Action Verb (AV), *base form, active voice*

The students / **add** their contribution to the school donation to Bantay Bukid.

The soldiers / **write** letters to their loved ones regularly.

The Present Time AV Phrase, HV + *past participle form, passive voice*

Their contribution / **is added** to the school donation to Bantay Bukid.

Letters / **are written** to their loved regularly by the soldiers.

1a) The Simple Present Time AV, -s, -*es form, active voice*

    He / **adds** his savings to the budget of his mother.

    Excelsa / **writes** articles for The Express.

The Present Time AV Phrase, HV + *past participle form, Passive Voice*

    His savings / **is added** to the budget of his mother.

    Articles / **are written** for the Express by Excelsa.

2) The Simple Past Time AV, *Active Voice*

    Mely / **added** some meat balls to the spaghetti her sister was cooking.

    Grego / **wrote** Delfina a letter.

The Past Time AV Phrase, *Passive Voice*

Some <u>meat balls</u> / **were added** to the spaghetti her sister was cooking by Mely..

A <u>letter</u> / **was written** to Delfina by Greg.

3) The Simple Future Time AV Phrase, *modal as helping verb*, *active voice*

The <u>students</u> / **will add** some amount to the school donation.

<u>Sheena</u> / **will write** an e-mail to her sister in Hong Kong.

The Future Time AV Phrase, *using modal & be verb*, *passive voice*

Some <u>amount</u> / **will be added** to the school donation by the students.

An <u>email</u> / **will be written** to her sister in Hong Kong by Sheena.

3a) The Future Time, *using the base form & appropriate adverbs showing futurity*, *active* voice

The airline <u>companies</u> / **add** additional flights *on Saturday*.

Lina and <u>Perla</u> / **write** letters to their husbands in Bacolod *tomorrow*.

The Future Time AV Phrase, *using verb phrases*, *passive voice*

Additional <u>flights</u> / **will be added** on *Saturday* by the company.

<u>Letters</u> / **will be written** to their husbands in Bacolod *tomorrow* by Lina and Perla.

4) The Present Progressive Time AV Phrase, using helping verb (HV + MV), *active voice*

<u>Marty</u> / **is adding** crushed pineapple to a salad mix.

<u>They</u> / **are writing** their assignments as we come home. The Present Progressive Time AV Phrase, *using helping verbs*, *passive voice*

Crushed <u>pineapple</u> / **is being added** to a salad mix by Marty.

Their <u>assignments</u> / **are being written** by them as we come home.

5) The Past Progressive Time AV Phrase, *active voice*

The <u>students</u> / **were adding** their contribution to the school donation to Bantay Bukid.

The <u>soldier</u> / **was writing** a letter to his mother.

The Past Progressive Time AV Phrase, *passive voice*

Their contribution / **was being added** to the school donation to Bantay Bukid.

A letter / **was being written** to his mother by the soldier.

6) The Future Progressive Time AV Phrase, *Active Voice*

The winners / **will be adding** feathers to their caps.

Ada / **will be writing** letters to her friends.

The Future Progressive Time AV Phrase, *passive voice*

Feathers / **will be being added** to their caps by the winners.

Letters / **will be being written** to her friends by Ada.

7) The Present Perfect Time AV Phrase, *active voice*

The girls / **have added** their share of the voluntary contribution to the Christmas party.

Jorge / **has written** his notes on the cover of his notebook.

The Present Perfect Time AV Phrase, *passive voice*

Their share of the voluntary contribution to the Christmas party / **have been added** by the girls.

His notes / **has been written** by Jorge on the cover of his notebook.

8) The Past Perfect Time AV Phrase, *active voice*

The laborers / **had added** sand to the concrete cement mixture.

Normita / **had written** their day's assignment on the chalkboard.

The Past Perfect Time AV Phrase, *passive voice*

Sand / **had been added** to the concrete cement mixture by the laborers.

Their day's assignment / **had been written** on the chalk board by Normita.

9) The Future Perfect Time AV Phrase, *active voice*

Cisco / **will have added** another degree to his name this March.

Dahlia / **will have written** her article for the Tribune today.

The Future Perfect Time AV Phrase, *passive voice*

Another degree to his name / **will have been added** by Cisco this March.

Her article for the Tribune today / **will have been written** by Dahlia.

10) The Present Perfect Progressive Time, *active voice*

The students / **have been adding** money to the donation pot.

Mary / **has been writing** her lesson plan for an hour now. The Present Perfect Progressive Time AV Phrase, *passive voice*

Money / **have been being added** to the donation pot by the students.

Her lesson plan / **has been being written** for an hour now by Mary.

11) The Past Perfect Progressive Time AV Phrase, *active voice*

The janitor / **had been adding** soil to the garden plot.

Maddela / **had been writing** slogans when I passed by her house.

The Past Perfect Progressive Time AV Phrase, *passive voice*

Soil / **had been being added** to the garden plot by the janitor.

Slogans / **had been being written** by Maddela when I passed by her house.

12) The Future Perfect Progressive Time, *active voice*

Cipriano / **will have been adding** amounts to his treasure chest.

The crewmen / **will have been writing** messages to their families on their kidnapping.

The Future Perfect Progressive Time AV Phrase, *passive voice*

Amounts / **will have been being added** by Cipriano to his treasure.

Messages on their kidnapping / **will have been being written** by the crewmen to their families.

A Sample Chart of the Five Basic Forms of Verb According to Time (Modern English Grammar)

Present Time		Past Time / (Past Participle*)	Past Participle**	Present Participle
1) base form	2) --s form	3) --ed form	4) --en form	5) --ing form
add* imply* write** hit** hang*(to execute / kill by hanging) hang**(to suspend) know** choose**	adds implies writes hits hangs hangs knows chooses	Added / (added*) implied wrote** hit** hanged hung** knew** chose**	written** hit** hung** known** chosen**	adding implying writing hitting hanging hanging knowing choosing

(Note: * = regular verb; ** = irregular verb)

o On the basis of the five forms of the modern English verb, words are identified as verbs or other parts of speech. The word **writ** is a *noun*, because it is *not one* of the *five forms* of the verb, which are (1) **base** form = **write**, (2) **--s** form = **writes**, (3) **--ed** form = **wrote**, (4) **--en** form = **written**, and (5) **--ing** form = **writing**. **Choice** is the noun of another irregular verb, **choose**. Its five verb forms are (1) **choose**, (2) **chooses**, (3) **chose**, (4) **chosen** and (5) **choosing**, in the order as indicated in the chart. **Addition** is the noun for the regular verb **add**; conjugated as (1) **add**, (2) **adds**, (3) **added**, (4) **added** and (5) **adding**.

○ Nouns may be derived from verbs, verbs from nouns and adjectives, and adjectives or adverbs from verbs and nouns, by simply adding / deleting derivational affixes, prefix and / or suffix. Both the prefix and suffix may be added to a word, as in enliven, which is live prefixed with letters en and a suffix n added at the end as verb. Other examples are: moan (N or V) = bemoan (V); live (V or Adj) = enliven (V); large (Adj) = enlarge (V); lucid (Adj) = elucidate (V) = lucidity (N); rail (N or V) = derail (V) = derailment (N); courage (N) = invalidate (V) = encouragement (N); timid (Adj) = intimidate (V); idol (N) = idolize (V) = idolized (V or Adj); strength (N) = strengthen (V); merry (Adj) = merrily (Adv) = merriment (N); valid (Adj) = validate (V) = validity(N)

• Being a part of speech, some words switch from one part of speech to another as they change in meaning and function. To function means "to serve in a particular capacity."

○ *Fast* is one word that has four roles or functions: 1) *noun*, 2) *verb*, 3) *adjective* and 4) *adverb*

    1) *Noun*: The fast of the strikers **/ ended** today.

    SN = *fast*, (the act of foregoing food or fasting)

    2) *Verb*: The Muslims / **fast** during the Ramadan.

    AV = *fast*, (to abstain from eating)

    3) *Adjective*: The horseracing enthusiast **/ brought** a *fast* steed

    Adj = *fast*, (rapid)

    4) *Adverb*: **/ Don't drive** your car too *fast* in congested areas.

    Adv = *fast*, (rapidly or speedily)

○ *Well* is another word that performs also four functions.

    1) *Noun*: Our village / **has** a deep *well*.

PN = *well*, (source of water)

2) *Verb*: <u>Tears</u> / **well** in her eyes as she embraced her long-lost mother.
                    ↑AV = *well*, (to rise from inner source)

3) *Adjective*: After a triumphant match, the <u>winner</u> \ **felt** quite *well*.
                                                    ↑   ↑
                                           LV   Adj = *well*, (in good health)

4) *Adverb*: The cultural <u>group</u> / **performed** *well*.
                                         AV↑   ↑
            Adv = *well*, (how the group performed)

◘ Clarification of the Twelve Times (Twelve Tenses) of the Verb

● That the English verb has twenty-four tenses can be clarified by using

1) the *active voice (the subject of the sentence is doing the action* or the sentence is in the Subject + Verb + Object or S + V + O Sentence Pattern) and

2) the *passive voice (the subject of the sentence is not doing the action but is being acted upon* or the sentence is in the Subject + Verb or S + V Sentence Pattern.

● *Only transitive verbs* in the S + V + O sentence pattern *can be transformed* from the *active* to the passive *voice*. An *intransitive verb, which may be in the active voice,* as in <u>He</u> /**eats** sparingly. (S + V pattern), *cannot be changed* into the *passive voice in the absence of an object* or *receiver of* the *action*, which will be the *subject* of the sentence in the *passive voice*. Note that the irregular verb **eat** is both *transitive* and *intransitive*.

● So far, we have not come across any reference that *contradicts* the aforementioned *perception*. Inasmuch as the *active voice differs from* the *passive voice as verb phrases* in the actual sentence construction, *each verb phrase in both the active and the passive voices represents one distinct tense*; hence, an English verb has *twenty-four tenses*.

    <u>Time</u> or <u>Tense</u> <u>Active Voice</u> <u>Passive Voice</u>

Subject + Verb + Object (S + V + O)   Subject + Verb (S + V)

1) The Present * = <u>He</u> / **eats** fruits. = <u>Fruits</u> / **are eaten** by him.

2) The Past * = <u>He</u> / ate fruits. = <u>Fruits</u> / **were eaten** by him.

3) The Future * = <u>He</u> / **will eat** fruits. = <u>Fruits</u> / **will be eaten** by him.

4) The Present Progressive = <u>He</u> / **is eating** fruits. = <u>Fruits</u> / **are being eaten** by him.

5) The Past Progressive = <u>He</u> / **was eating** fruits. = <u>Fruits</u> / **were being eaten** by him.

6) The Future Progressive = <u>He</u> / **will be eating** fruits. = <u>Fruits</u> / **will be being eaten** by him.

7) The Present Perfect = He / **has eaten** fruits. = <u>Fruits</u> / **have been eaten** by him.

8) The Past Perfect = <u>He</u> / **had eaten** fruits. = <u>Fruits</u> / **had been eaten** by him.

9) The Future Perfect = <u>He</u> / **will have eaten** fruits.= <u>Fruits</u> / **will have been eaten** by him.

10) The Present Perfect Progressive = <u>He</u> / **has been eating** fruits. = <u>Fruits</u> / **have been being eaten** by him.

11) The Past Perfect Progressive = <u>He</u> / **had been eating** fruits. = <u>Fruits</u> / **had been being eaten** by him.

12) The Future Perfect Progressive = <u>He</u> / **will have been eating** fruits.= <u>Fruits</u> / **will have been eaten** by him.

☐ The "Twenty-Four Tenses" of the English Verb, Explained In Various Sentence Examples

• 1. The *Simple Present Time* Action Verbs (AV), *Active Voice* = **design / lends**

◊ 1a) The <u>students</u> / **design** chairs at the local high school.
↑   ↑   ↑ O = Object or direct object
= *chairs*

SN, plural　　　　　　AV, regular, **base** form, simple present time, *active voice* = **design,** agreeing with plural SN = students

◊ 1b) Fred / **lends** a bicycle to Owen.
　　　↑　　　↑　　　　　O

SN, singular　　AV, irregular, --**s** form, simple present time, active voice = **lends** (V base form = *lend*), agreeing with singular SN = Fred

- 2. The *Present Time* AV Phrases, *Passive Voice* = **are designed / is lent**

◊ 2a) Chairs / **are designed** by the students at the local high school.
　　　↑　　　↑　　↑

　　　　　　MV, --**ed** form, past participle = **designed** (V base form = SN, plural *design*)

　　　　　　HV, present time = **are** (HV = *be*), agreeing with plural SN = chairs

◊ 2b) A bicycle / **is lent** to Owen by Fred.
　　　↑　　　↑　↑

　　　　　　MV, irregular, --**en** form, past participle = **lent** (V base form = SN, singular *lend*)

　　　　　　HV, present time = **is** (HV = *be*), agreeing with singular SN= bicycle

- 3. The *Simple Past Time* Action Verbs, *Active Voice* = **served / won**

◊ 3a) Neil / **served** the Army for twenty–five years.
　　　↑　　　↑

　　SN, singular　　AV, regular, --**ed** form, simple past time, active voice = **served** (V base form =*serve*)

◊ 3b) Roy / **won** a car in a raffle.
　　　↑　　　↑
`　　SN, singular　　AV, irregular, --**en** form, simple past time, active voice = **won** (V base form = *win*)

- 4. The *Past Time* AV Phrases, *Passive Voice* = **was served** / **was won**

  ◊ 4a) The Army / **was served** for twenty-five years by Neil.
  SN,

  AV,--**ed** form, past participle=served (V base form= *serve*)

  singular HV, past time = **was** (HV = *be*), agreeing with singular SN =Army

  ◊ 4b) A car / **was won** by Roy in a raffle.
  SN, singular

AV, irregular, --**en** form, past participle = **won** (V base form = *win*)

HV, past time = **was** (HV = *be*), agreeing with singular SN = car

- 5. The *Simple Future Time* AV Phrases, *Active Voice* = **will sing** / **shall report**

  ◊ 5a) The soldiers / **will sing** Christmas songs in their graduation program.

  SN, plural   MV, **base** form, simple present time = **sing**

  HVM, present time = **will** (HV = *modal*), *indicating simple futurity*

  ◊ 5b) The scouts / **shall report** their reconnaissance to the commander.

  SN, plural

  MV, regular, **base** form, simple present time = **report**

  HVM, present time = **shall** (HV = *modal*), *indicating obligation*

- 6.The *Simple Future Time* AV Phrases, *Passive Voice* = **will be sung / shall be reported**

◊ 6a) Christmas songs / **will be sung** by the soldiers in their graduation program.

    SN, plural   MV, --**en** form, past participle = **sung** (V base form = HVM, present time = **will** (HV *sing*)

= *modal*), *indicating futurity*   HV, present form = **be** (HV = be)

◊ 6b) The reconnaissance / **shall be reported** by the scouts to the commander.

    SN, singular   MV, --**ed** form, past participle = **reported**

    HVM, present time = **shall** —— (V base form = *report*)

    (HV = *modal*) showing obligation   HV, present form = **be** (HV = *be*)

- 7. The *Present Progressive Time* AV Phrases, *Active Voice* = **is painting / are reading**

◊ 7a) Richard / **is painting** a portrait.

    SN, singular

    MV, --**ing** form, present participle **painting** (V base form = *paint*)

    HV, present time = **is** (HV = *be*), agreeing with singular SN = Richard

◊ 7b) They / **are reading** science books.

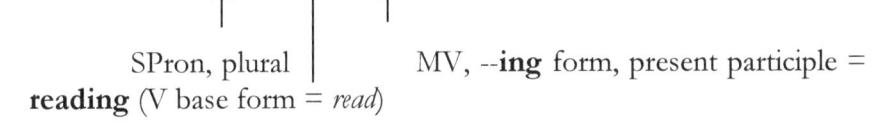

    SPron, plural   MV, --**ing** form, present participle = **reading** (V base form = *read*)

HV, present time = **are** (HV = *be*), agreeing with plural SPron = they

●8. The *Present Progressive Time* AV Phrases, *Passive Voice* = **is being painted / are being read**

◊ 8a) A portrait / **is being painted** by Richard.

         MV,--**ed** form, past participle = **painted** (V base form =

SN, singular *paint*)

MHV, present time =   HV, --**ing** form, present participle = **being** (HV = *be*)

is (HV = *be*), agreeing with singular SN = portrait

◊ 8b) Science books / **are being read** by them.

         MV, --**en** form, past participle = **read** (V base form

SN, plural   = *read*)

MHV, present time = **are** — HV, --**ing** form, present participle = **being** (HV = *be*)

(HV = *be*), agreeing with plural SN = science books

●9. The *Past Progressive Time* AV Phrases, *Active Voice* = **was building / were solving**

◊ 9a) Jun / **was building** a birdhouse when his guests came.

SN, singular   MV, irregular, --**ing** form, present participle = **building** (V base form = *build*)

HV, past time = **was** (HV = *be*), agreeing with singular SN = Jun

◊ 9b) The children / were solving puzzles.

      SN, plural   MV, regular, --**ing** form, present participle = **solving**

(V base form = *solve*)

                    HV, past time = **were** (HV = *be*), agreeing with plural SN = children

●10. The *Past Progressive Time* AV Phrases, *Passive Voice* = **was being built / were being**

    solved

      ◊ 10a) A birdhouse / **was being built** by Jun when his guests came.

      SN, singular   MV, --**en** form, past participle = **built** (V base form

                                              =*build*)

      MHV, past time = **was**   HV, --**ing** form, present participle = **being** (HV = *be*)

    (HV = *be*), agreeing with singular SN = birdhouse

    ◊ 10b) Puzzles / **were being solved** by the children.

      SN, plural   MV, --**ed** form, past participle = **solved** (V base form

                                      =*solve*)

HV, past time = **were** (HV = _)   MHV, --**ing** form, present participle = **being** (HV = *be*)

  be), agreeing with plural SN = puzzles

●11. The *Future Progressive Time* AV Phrases, *Active Voice* = **will be running / will be starring**

◊ 11a) Grace / **will be running** the fiesta.
SN, singular   MV, --**ing** form, present participle
= **running** (V base form
                          = *run*)
HVM, present ~~time~~ =   MHV, present time = **be** (HV = *be*)
will (HV=*modal*)

◊ 11b) Brian / **will be starring** in a comedy during the festival.
SN, singular   MV, --**ing** form, present
participle = **starring** (V base
                          form = *star*)
HVM, present time =   ___ **MHV,** present time = **be** (HV = *be*)
will (HV=*modal*)

• 12. The *Future Progressive Time* AV Phrases, *Passive Voice* = **will be being run / will be being starred**

◊ 12a) The fiesta / **will be being run** by Grace.
SN, singular   MV, --**en** form, past
participle= **run** (V base form =
                          run)
HVM, present ~~time~~ = **will**   MHV, present participle = **being** (HV = *be*)
(HV=*modal*)   HV, present form = **be** (HV = *be*)

◊ 12b) A show / **will be being starred** in by Brian.
SN, singular   MV, --**ed** form, past
participle = **starred** (V base
                          form = *star*)
HVM, present time = **will**   MHV, present participle = **being**
(HV = *be*
(HV=*modal*)   HV, present form = **be** (HV = *be*)

●13. The *Present Perfect Time* AV Phrases, *Active Voice* = **has left** / **has explored**

◊ 13a) <u>Sam</u> / **has left** his estate in the care of Joe.

SN, singular base form = *leave*)   MV, --**en** form, past participle = **left** (V

HV, present time = **has** (HV = *have*), agreeing with singular SN = <u>Sam</u>

◊ 13b) <u>Ike</u> / **has explored** some caves.

SN, singular   MV, --**ed** form, past participle = **explored** (V base form = *explore*)   HV, present time = **has** (HV = *have*), agreeing with singular SN = <u>Ike</u>

●14. The *Present Perfect Time* AV Phrases, *Passive Voice* = **has been left** / **have been explored**

◊ 14a) His <u>estate</u> / **has been left** in the care of Joe by Sam.

SN, singular   MV, --**en** form, past participle = **left** (V base form =

leave)

HV, present ~~time~~ = **has**   MHV, --**en** form, past participle= **been** (HV = *be*)

(HV = *have*), agreeing with singular SN = <u>estate</u>

◊ 14b) Some <u>caves</u> / **have been explored** by Ike.

SN, plural participle = **explored** (V base   MV, --**ed** form, past

HV, present time = **have**   form = *explore*)

(HV = have), agreeing   MHV, --en form, past participle e= **been** (HV = *be*)

with plural SN = <u>caves</u>

●15. The *Past Perfect Time* AV Phrases, *Active Voice* = **had given / had invested**

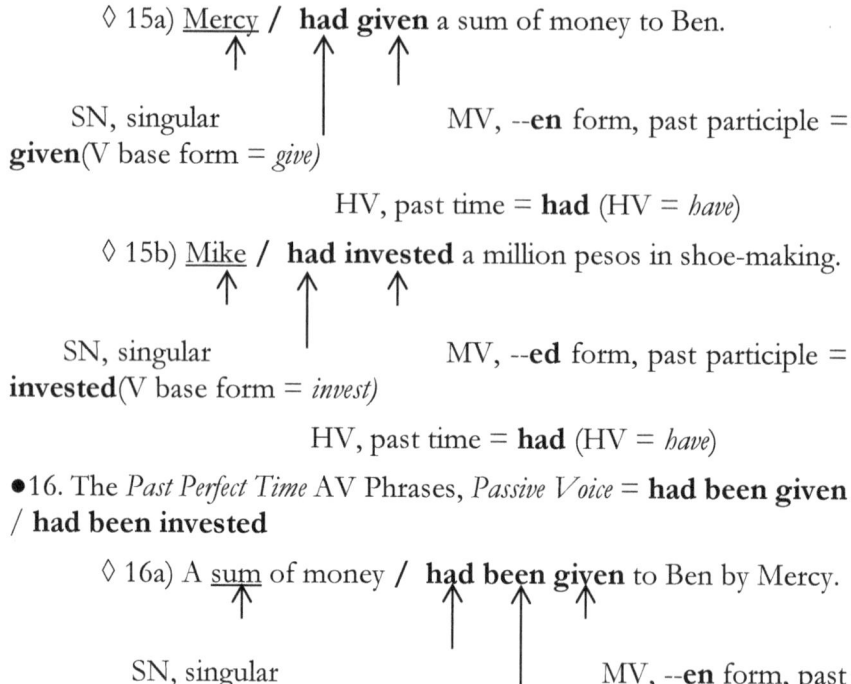

◊ 15a) <u>Mercy</u> **/ had given** a sum of money to Ben.

SN, singular   MV, --**en** form, past participle = **given**(V base form = *give)*

HV, past time = **had** (HV = *have)*

◊ 15b) <u>Mike</u> **/ had invested** a million pesos in shoe-making.

SN, singular   MV, --**ed** form, past participle = **invested**(V base form = *invest)*

HV, past time = **had** (HV = *have)*

●16. The *Past Perfect Time* AV Phrases, *Passive Voice* = **had been given / had been invested**

◊ 16a) A <u>sum</u> of money **/ had been given** to Ben by Mercy.

SN, singular   MV, --**en** form, past participle = **given** (V base form = *give*)

HV, past time = **had** (HV = *have)*

MHV, --**en** form, past participle = **been** (HV = *be)*

◊ 16b) A <u>million pesos</u> **/ had been invested** by Mike in shoe-making.

SN, singular participle = **invested**

MV, --**ed** form, (V base form = *invest)*

HV, past time = **had** (HV = *have*   MHV, --**en** form, past participle = **been** (HV = *be)*

●17. The *Future Perfect Time* AV Phrases, *Active Voice* = **wll have married / will have taken**

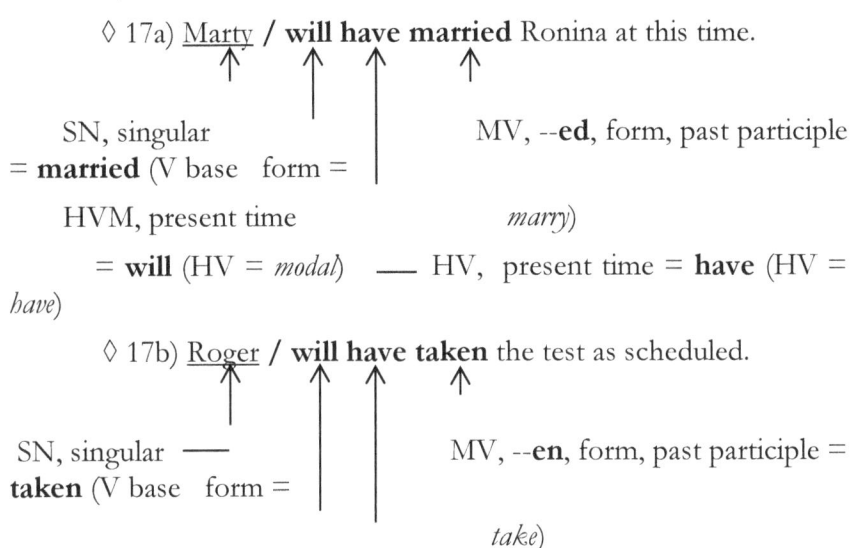

    ◊ 17a) Marty **/ will have married** Ronina at this time.

SN, singular   MV, --**ed**, form, past participle
= **married** (V base form =

    HVM, present time   *marry*)

    = **will** (HV = *modal*) ⎯⎯ HV, present time = **have** (HV = *have*)

    ◊ 17b) Roger **/ will have taken** the test as scheduled.

SN, singular ⎯⎯   MV, --**en**, form, past participle =
taken (V base form =

                                                take)

    HVM, present time

    = **will** (HV = *modal*)   HV, present time = **have** (HV = *have*)

●18. The *Future Perfect Time* AV Phrases, *Passive Voice* = **will have been married / will have been taken**

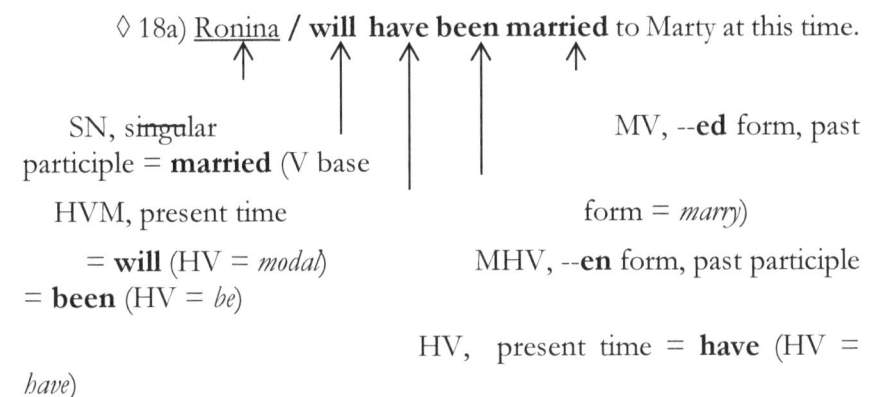

    ◊ 18a) Ronina **/ will have been married** to Marty at this time.

SN, singular   MV, --**ed** form, past
participle = **married** (V base

    HVM, present time   form = *marry*)

    = **will** (HV = *modal*)   MHV, --**en** form, past participle
= **been** (HV = *be*)

                            HV, present time = **have** (HV = *have*)

    ◊ 18b) The test **/ will have been taken** by Roger as scheduled.

SN, singular ——— MV, --**en** form, past participle= **taken** (V base form

HVM, present time = = *take*)

will (HV = *modal*) MHV, --**en** form, past participle = **been** (HV = *be*)

HV, present time = **have** (HV = *have*)

●19. The *Present Perfect Progressive Time* AV Phrases, *Active Voice* = **has been reading / have been herding**

◊ 19a) Clyde **/ has been reading** books all day.

SN, singular MV, --**ing** form, present participle = **reading** (V base form

= *read*)

HV, present time ——— MHV, past participle = **been** (HV = *be*)

has (HV = *have*), agreeing with singular SN = Clyde

◊ 19b) The boys **/ have been herding** carabaos in the fields.

SN, plural ——— MV, --**ing** form, present participle = **herding**

HV, present time = ——— (V base form = *herd*)

have (HV = *have*), MHV, past participle =**been** (HV = *be*)

agreeing with plural SN = boys

●20. The *Present Perfect Progressive Time* AV Phrases, *Passive Voice* = **have been being read / have been being herded**

◊ 20a) Books **/ have been being read** all day by Clyde.

SN, plural participle = **read** (V base form = *read*)

(HV = *have*), agreeing participle = **being** (HV = *be*)

with plural SN = books (HV = *be*)

MV, --**en** form, past HV1, present time = **have**

MHV, --**ing** form, present

HV2, --**en** form, past participle = **been**

◊ 20b) <u>Carabaos</u> **/ have been being herded** in the fields by the boys.

SN, plural participle **herded** (V base

HV1, present time = time **have** (HV = *have*) participle = **being** (HV = *be*) **been** (HV = *be*)

MV, --**ed** form, past

form = *herd*)

MHV, --**ing** form, present HV2, --**en** form, past participle =

agreeing with plural SN = <u>carabaos</u>

●21. The *Past Perfect Progressive Time* AV Phrases, *Active Voice* = **had been caring / had been sweeping**

◊ 21a) Zinnia **/ had been caring** for her sick mother until her sister took over.

SN, singular = **caring**

HV, past time = **had**

(HV = *have*)

be)

MV, --**ing** form, present participle

(V base form = *care*)

MHV, past participle = **been** (HV =

◊ 21b) <u>Nadia</u> **/ had been sweeping** their yard before the rain came.

SN, singular = **sweeping**

MV, --**ing** form, present participle

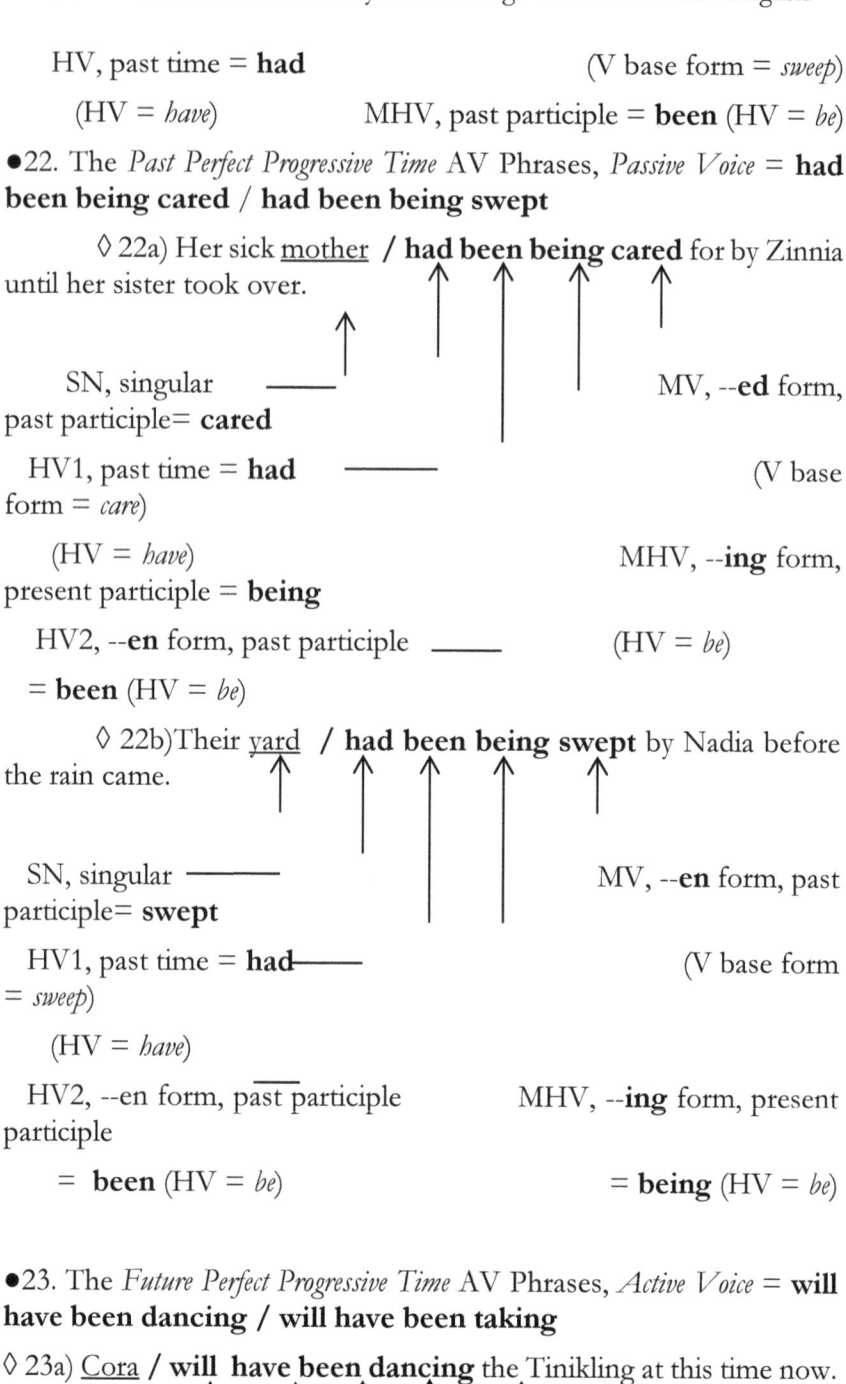

HV, past time = **had**   (V base form = *sweep*)

(HV = *have*)   MHV, past participle = **been** (HV = *be*)

●22. The *Past Perfect Progressive Time* AV Phrases, *Passive Voice* = **had been being cared / had been being swept**

◊ 22a) Her sick mother / **had been being cared** for by Zinnia until her sister took over.

SN, singular past participle= **cared**   MV, --**ed** form,

HV1, past time = **had**   (V base form = *care*)

(HV = *have*)   MHV, --**ing** form, present participle = **being**

HV2, --**en** form, past participle   (HV = *be*)

= **been** (HV = *be*)

◊ 22b)Their yard / **had been being swept** by Nadia before the rain came.

SN, singular participle= **swept**   MV, --**en** form, past

HV1, past time = **had**   (V base form = *sweep*)

(HV = *have*)

HV2, --**en** form, past participle   MHV, --**ing** form, present participle

= **been** (HV = *be*)   = **being** (HV = *be*)

●23. The *Future Perfect Progressive Time* AV Phrases, *Active Voice* = **will have been dancing / will have been taking**

◊ 23a) Cora / **will have been dancing** the Tinikling at this time now.

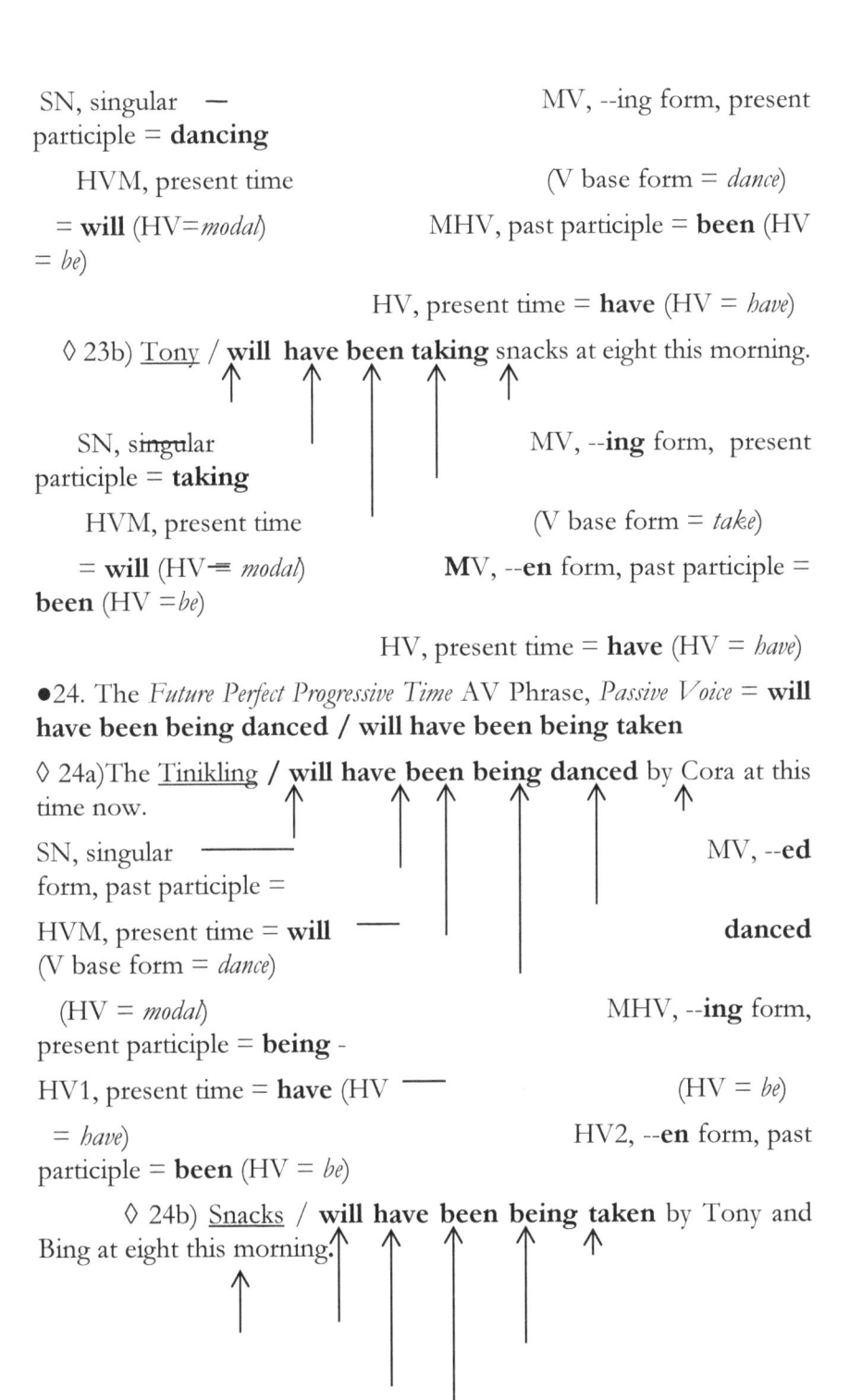

SN, singular — 　　　　　　　　MV, --ing form, present
participle = **dancing**

　HVM, present time　　　　　　(V base form = *dance*)

　= **will** (HV=*modal*)　　　MHV, past participle = **been** (HV
= *be*)

　　　　　　　　　HV, present time = **have** (HV = *have*)

◊ 23b) <u>Tony</u> / **will have been taking** snacks at eight this morning.

　SN, singular　　　　　　　　　MV, --**ing** form, present
participle = **taking**

　HVM, present time　　　　　　(V base form = *take*)

　= **will** (HV= *modal*)　　　MV, --**en** form, past participle =
been (HV =*be*)

　　　　　　　　　HV, present time = **have** (HV = *have*)

●24. The *Future Perfect Progressive Time* AV Phrase, *Passive Voice* = **will have been being danced / will have been being taken**

◊ 24a)The <u>Tinikling</u> / **will have been being danced** by Cora at this time now.

SN, singular ——— 　　　　　　　　　　　　　MV, --**ed**
form, past participle =

HVM, present time = **will** ———　　　　　　　　**danced**
(V base form = *dance*)

　(HV = *modal*)　　　　　　　　　MHV, --**ing** form,
present participle = **being** -

HV1, present time = **have** (HV ——　　　　　(HV = *be*)

= *have*)　　　　　　　　　　　　　HV2, --**en** form, past
participle = **been** (HV = *be*)

　　◊ 24b) <u>Snacks</u> / **will have been being taken** by Tony and Bing at eight this morning.

SN, plural
participle = **taken**

HVM, present time = **will** *take*)

(HV = *modal*)
participle = **being** (HV =

HV1, present time = **have**——

(HV = *have*)
= **been** (HV = *be*)

MV, --**en** form, past

(V base form =

MHV, --**ing** form, present

be)

HV2, --**en** form, past participle

☐ Exercise 15 : Identify the *voice* of each sentence whether *active* or *passive*.

1. Mr. <u>Grande</u> / **is supported** by the party.
2. A new <u>car</u> / **was bought** by Hermes.
3. <u>Wages</u> / **will be paid** on weekly basis by the manager.
4. A <u>cake</u> / **is being baked** by the girls.
5. <u>Hermes</u> / **bought** a new car.
6. The <u>manager</u> / **will pay** wages on weekly basis.
7. <u>Dresses</u> / **were being sewn** by the women.
8. The <u>girls</u> / **are baking** a cake.
9. <u>Accounting</u> / **will be being studied** in London by Maria.
10. The <u>committee</u> / **have known** the candidate for a long time.
11. The <u>candidate</u> / **has been known** by the committee for a long time.
12. The <u>board</u> / **had dismissed** the guard for gross neglect of duties.
13. The <u>party</u> / **supports** Mr. Grande.
14. The <u>women</u> / **were sewing** dresses.
15. <u>Maria</u> / **will be studying** accounting in London.

16. Sam / **will have finished** his project.

17. Deo / **has been raking** leaves in the garden.

18. Carl / **had been singing** hymns.

19. The guard / **had been dismissed** by the board for gross neglect of duties.

20. His project / **will have been finished** by Sam.

21. Leaves / **have been being raked** in the garden by Deo.

22. Hymns / **had been being sung** by Carl.

23. The Cariñosa / **will have been being danced** by Rex.

24. She / **was elected** member of the parliament.

☐ Exercise 16 : List down the *active* and *passive* AV phrases used in sentences

1. Ciara and Clara / are nominated to the barangay council.

2. The scouter / is mistaken for being an enemy of the rebels.

3. An error / was corrected by the teacher at once.

4. The Tigers / were beaten by the Lions.

5. His field / will be planted to corn.

6. The goods / will be sold to poultry farmers.

7. Some girls / are baking a cake.

8. The women / were sewing dresses.

9. Maria / will be enrolling in medical technology.

10. The council / have nullified the resolution authorizing gambling operation.

11. The committee / have known the candidate for a long time.

12. The board / had dismissed the guard for being grossly negligent of his duties.

13. The party / had withdrawn its support for the erring candidate.

14. Sam / should have voted in the elections if he had been home.

15. Rey / should have taken the test to qualify for promotion.

16. <u>Joe</u> / has been raking leaves in the garden.
17. The <u>men</u> / have been plowing their farms.
18. <u>Carl</u> / had been singing hymns.
19. <u>Rex</u> / shall have been dancing the Tinikling.
20. The show / shall have been being presented by the group.

☐ Additional Details in the Study of the Structure of the English Grammar

• The following must be studied in conjunction with the preceding discussion. It is not a repetition, but an "expanded" explanation that may help one in using correctly the English language.

☐ Sentence Order

○ Normal Order. – Usually, the sentences are constructed with the subject appearing before the predicate.

◊ <u>The economy of the Philippines</u> \ **is** on its way to recovery from a slump.

(The *complete subject* or *noun phrase* = <u>The economy of the Philippines</u>; the *complete predicate* or verb phrase = ***is*** *on its way to recovery from a slump*.)

○ Reverse Order. Sentences in the reverse order abound in literary works like poetry, plays, etc.

◊ All alone **am** \ <u>I</u>.

(*Complete* su*b*ject = <u>I</u>; complete predicate = ***am*** *all alone*.)

◊ Music to her ears **was** \ the plaintive <u>cry</u> of her newborn.

(*Complete subject* = the plaintive <u>cry</u> of her newborn; *complete* pred*i*cate = ***was***

music to her ears)

◊ Boom! **sounded** / the first <u>bomb</u> of the Liberation forces.

(*Complete subject* = the first <u>bomb</u> of the Liberation forces; *complete predicate* =

sounded *boom*)

☐ Compound Subject and Compound Predicate of a Sentence

○ A compound subject consists of two or more subjects – two nouns or pronouns or noun phrases joined by a conjunction *and* or with modifiers – that tell who or what the sentence is about.

◊ <u>Lara</u> and <u>Romeo</u> \ **are** siblings. <u>She</u> and <u>he</u> were adopted by two wealthy families.

(Compound subject N = <u>Lara *and* Romeo</u>); <u>(Compound subject Pron = She and he)</u>

◊ Swaying <u>clumps</u> of bamboos, imposing <u>acacia</u> and fruit-bearing <u>mango trees</u> /

beautify Lolita's farm.

(Complete compound subjects = <u>swaying clumps of bamboos, imposing acacia *and*</u>

<u>fruit-bearing mango trees</u>)

○ A compound predicate, which describes action or states condition of the subject, is made up of two or more simple predicates or verb phrases joined by the conjunction *and*.

◊ The soldiers / **ran, crouched** and **took** cover.

(Complete compound predicates = **ran, crouched** *and* **took** cover)

◊ The protesters / **chanted** slogans, **burned** effigies, and **taunted** the tolerant

policemen.

(Complete compound predicates = **chanted** slogans, **burned** effigies *and* **taunted**

the tolerant policemen)

☐ Exercise 17 : Separate the *complete subject* from the *complete* predicate by copying on your paper the words comprising the two parts, each part on separate line.

1. Typhoon Ruping destroyed many houses.

2. One cold December morning, Rosendo went up the mountain.

3. The mayor was disappointed with the action of the city council.

4. The policeman was commended posthumously for bravery.

5. Cutting across the plains, the safari crossed the turbulent river before the rains.

6. Who was Simon Peter?

7. Ailing for ten years, his grandfather died on his wedding day.

8. Terry lost her valuables to the fire that gutted their house.

9. The candidate for Miss Dinagyang did not win despite spending a big amount of money.

10. Having been sent to prison for murder, Celso reformed and became a Baptist minister.

☐ Exercise 18 : On your paper, write the *subjects* (simple or compound) and the *predicates* (simple or compound) of the following sentences.

1. The versatile actress sang and danced in the show.

2. Tall buildings, fast cars and elevated trains are indicators of progress.

3. The boy scouts who were hungry, weary and sleepy returned to the camp.

4. How could I have gone there!

5. Rodolfo and I wrote Margarita, Susana and Lucila in Manila.

6. Roses, orchids, poinsettia and gladioli are some of the plants in Carlo's garden.

7. The wayward car, driven by a crazed man, screeched, honked, revved up and crashed against other vehicles before being stopped by a thick wall.

8. Muscular boys, giggling girls, brusque thugs and pious men were seen joining the merrymaking in commemoration of the independence of the new nation.

9. Porthos laughed, jumped, shouted and dashed around the house after he won the lottery.

10. Raizza, Karen, Lily and Kaya went to Boracay to celebrate their graduation from college.

☐ Placement of Subject and Predicate of a Sentence

- Declarative Sentence – The *subject* usually precedes the *predicate* in a declarative sentence.

◊ Bananas / **abound** in Benigno's orchard. (Subject = Bananas; predicate = **abound** in Benigno's orchard)

o When some form of emphasis comes under consideration, like habit or peculiarities, the *predicate* appears before the *subject* in the sentence.

◊ Under the branch **hang** / the bats

(Predicate = **hang** under the branch; subject = the bats)

o When the adverb *here* or *there* is an *expletive*, the *predicate* comes ahead of the *subject*.

◊ *There* **are** \ the cars that collided against each other.

(Complete predicate = **are** *there* ; complete subject = the cars that collided against each other)

- Interrogative Sentence – The *subject* usually appears *between* the *two parts* of the *verb phrase*.

◊ **Have** you **completed** your work?

(Simple subject = you ; predicate = **have completed**)

◊ **Is** it all right? (Simple subject = it ; predicate = **is**)

(Raising the voice at the end of a statement makes it interrogative = You / have

completed your work?   It \ is all right?

- Imperative Sentence – The *subject* you is usually implied or understood or not stated. It is also understood that the *subject* in an imperative sentence (direct order) is the *pronoun* **you**.

◊ Please **get** out of his way.

(You / **get** out of his way, please.)

◊ **Submit** your term paper tomorrow.

(You / **submit** your term paper tomorrow.)

- Exclamatory Sentence – Usually, the subject precedes the predicate, except when the sentence is a very emphatic and imperative one.

◊ Mea culpa! I \ **am** sorry for all the troubles!
◊ **/ Don't panic.   / Go** this way!

(*Not* is an adverb, however, in contraction it becomes part of the verb.)

☐ Verb and Verb Phrases

• The structure of the sentence that functions as the predicate is the *verb* or *verb phrase*. The verb phrase is also referred to as the *complete predicate*, which phrase consists of the verb and all the words that follow it, including adverbs that may be found in the subject and set off by a comma.

◊ *Inadvertently*, Mr. Lopez / **included** his name in the blacklist.

(The complete predicate or the complete verb phrase = **included** *his name in the blacklist* includes the adverb *inadvertently* that introduces emphatically the sentence.)

◊ We / **have been planting** trees since June.

(The verb phrase of three words, **have been planting**, shows action; the complete predicate is ***have been planting*** *trees since June*.)

☐ Verb Phrase and Complements

• A complement or completer is the idea or thing that completes or brings the predicate to perfection. A word or group of words that completes the meaning of the predicate of a sentence is called *complement*.

◊ The victory of the troops / **surprised** the *general*.

(complement = *general, direct object* of the verb = **surprised**.)

• There are five different kinds of complements: 1) direct object (DO), 2) indirect object (IO), 3) objective complement (OC) and 4) predicate nominative (PN) and predicate adjective (PA). The first three are *objects* (O) and the last two are *subject complements* (SC).

• 1) *Direct Objects* (DO). A direct object (DO) is a noun, pronoun or group of words acting as a noun that receives the action of a transitive verb (indicated as *v.t.* in the dictionary). The transitive verb is an action verb (AV) in the active voice and answers the question *what?* or *whom?*

Modifiers are not part of the direct object, they are completers or they complete or complement ideas. Used with transitive verbs, direct objects (DO) complete the predicates by receiving actions from the verbs. Transitive verbs carry action across to the objects.

Sentence Pattern: SUBJECT + VERB + OBJECT (S + V + O or S + AV + O)

◊ Elsa / **wrote** a *letter.*
SN AV DO (The action verb (AV) = **wrote** is a *transitive verb,* that is, it carries the action of the subject (S) = Elsa to the direct object (DO) = *letter.*)

◊ Guia / **prepares** the *commencement program* of the school.
SN AV DO (Prepares *what?* Answer = *commencement program*)

◊ Arnulfo / **gave** Lea a *bouquet* of roses.
SN AV DO (Gave *what?* Answer = *bouquet*)

◊ The principal / **commended** him *an industrious man.*
SN AV DO (Commended *whom?* Answer = *an industrious man*)

o The sentence has an *intransitive* verb; it has no object. (Sentence Pattern : S + V)

◊ Crisanto / **swam** in the sea.

(**swam** has no receiver; *sea* is not the object of **swam**, but of the preposition *in;* Prep.

phrase *in the sea* is an adverb modifying the *intransitive* verb **swam**)

• 2) *Indirect Objects* (IO). *Noun phrases* following the *transitive* verbs are called objects of the verbs. The two kinds of objects are direct and indirect objects.

• An indirect object (IO) is a noun or pronoun that comes after the action verb and before a direct object (DO). It names the person or thing that something is given to or done for. (Symbol: IO). Sentence

Pattern Three: SUBJECT + ACTION VERB + INDIRECT OBJECT + DIRECT OBJECT or S + AV + IO + DO

○ Indirect object (IO) = *us* (The action of Miss Gonzales is directed to *us*.) ; S + AV + IO + DO

◊ <u>Miss Gonzales</u> **/ teaches** *us* Filipino.
       ↑   ↑   ↑   ↑
   SN   AV   IO   DO or O

◊ <u>Priscilla</u> **/ left** *Hernando* a hundred pesos.
 ↑   ↑   ↑   ↑
SN   AV   IO   DO (A hundred pesos was given to *Hernando*.

◊ <u>Mateo</u> **/ bought** his brother a *jacket*.
↑SN   ↑AV   ↑IO   ↑DO (*jacket* is the receiver of **bought**, as AV)

◊ <u>Mateo</u> **/ bought** a *jacket* for Claudio.
↑   ↑   ↑
S   AV   DO

(*Claudio* is the object of Prep = *for*, not an indirect object ; Prep phrase = *for Claudio*, an *adjective* modifying *jacket*.)

• 3) *Objective Complements (OC).* An objective complement (OC) is a noun, adjective or group of words acting as a noun that follows a direct object and describes or renames it and completes the meaning of the direct object (DO).

◊ The <u>school administrator</u> **/ designated** Roberto *commandant* of the cadets.   ↑   ↑   ↑   ↑
                 SN   AV   DO   OC

Prep phrase = *of* the cadets

◊ My <u>niece</u> **/ named** her baby *Raizza*.
↑   ↑   ↑   ↑
SN   AV   DO OC

• Objective complements (OC) may be determined by stating the verb and the direct object and then ask what completes the idea presented.

◊ The <u>supervisor</u> / **considered** Peregrina *lazy*.
SN⋀ AV⋀ DO⋀ OC⋀ (Adj = *lazy* completing idea given by the verb.)

○ An objective complement (OC) may be in compound structure.

◊ The <u>mayor</u> / **appointed** Mimosa as personal *secretary* and *chief* of the administrative staff.

⋀ ⋀ ⋀ ⋀ ⋀
SN AV DO OC OC

• 4) *Subject Complements*. A subject complement (*completer*) is the noun, pronoun or adjective after follows a linking verb and tells something about the subject of the sentence. A predicate nominative is a noun that follows a linking verb and renames, identifies, or explains the subject of the sentence. Two kinds of subject complements: predicate nominative or predicate noun (PN) and predicate adjective (PA).

◊ <u>Senator Franklin Drilon</u> \ **is** the *President* of the Philippine Senate.
⋀ SN⋀ LV⋀ PN⋀

• A predicate adjective follows a linking verb and describes the subject of the sentence.

◊ The <u>car</u> \ **was** *classy*.
SN⋀ LV⋀ PA⋀   ⋀

◊ That <u>part</u> of the zigzag road \ **appeared** *hazardous*.

⋀ ⋀ ⋀ ⋀ ⋀ ⋀
SN LV PA SN LV PA

• A sentence may have compound complements.

◊ <u>Ann Lyra Mae</u> \ **sounded** nervously *excited* but *happy*.
SN⋀ AV or LV⋀ PA⋀ PA⋀

◊ A <u>boy</u> named Manuel \ **became** a *general* and *president* of his country.
SN⋀ LV⋀ PN⋀ PN⋀

• *Be as Linking Verb Followed by a Phrase as Completer*. A linking verb <u>be</u> cannot stand alone as an idea; it needs a *completer* (noun, adjective or adverb). (Sentence Pattern Four: SUBJECT + LINKING VERB +

NOUN or S + LV + N, and variants, S + LV + ADJ and S + LV + ADV).

- *Noun* (N) completer = *lady*   (S + LV + N)
- ◊ The <u>doctor</u> \ **is** a *lady*.
        SN   LV   N

completer or complement (PN) = *lady*

- *Adjective* (Adj) completer = *wet*   (S + LV + Adj)
- ◊ The <u>carolers</u> \ **were** *wet*.
        SN   LV   Adj,

completer or complement (PA) = *wet*

- *Adverb* (Adv) completer = *at the door*   (S + LV + Adv)
- ◊ Your <u>friends</u> \ **are** *at the door*.
        SN   LV   Adv,

completer = *at the door* (Prep phrase)

- *Intransitive* and *Transitive Verbs – Their Differences*

- The *intransitive* verb needs *no completer* or *object*, whereas the *transitive* verb *cannot stand alone without* the *completer* or *object*. An *intransitive verb* (**v. i.**) expresses a complete statement. It is not "in transit" (going) to anywhere, but by itself it tells the whole story. The intransitive verb falls under the Sentence Pattern SUBJECT + VERB or S + V. However, for "effects" or "colors," *adverbs* of *manner* (how), *place* (where), and *time* (when) follow intransitive verbs.

- Intransitive V = **sings** (basic intransitive)
- ◊ <u>Eva</u> / **sings**. [S + V]
    SN,   AV, irregular, v. i., --s form, present time = **sings** (V base form = *sing*)   singular
- Intransitive V = **worked**, with adverb of *manner* = *quickly*
- ◊ 2) <u>Neren</u> / **worked** *quickly*. S + V]

SN, singular   [Adv (of *manner*) = *quickly*, modifying
AV = **worked**]

AV, regular, **v. i.**, --**ed** form, past time = **worked** (V base form = *work*)

○ Intransitive V = **looked**, with adverb of *place* (prepositional phrase) = *in the convents*

◊ The <u>detectives</u> **/ looked** *in the convents.* [S + V]
                ↑   ↑
                             [Adv (of place) = *in the convents*, modifying AV = **looked**]
        SN, plural   AV, regular, **v. i.**, --**ed** form, past time = **looked** (V base form = *look*)

○ Intransitive V = **prays**, with adverb of *time* (prep phrase) = *at three o'clock in the afternoon*

◊ <u>She</u> **/ prays** *at three o'clock in the afternoon.* [S + V]
        ↑   ↑
SPron,   [Adv = *at three o'clock in the afternoon*, modifying AV = **prays**]
    singular   AV, regular, **v. i.**, –**s** form, present time, = **prays** (V base form = *pray*),
            agreeing with singular SPron = <u>she</u>

● The *transitive verb (**v.t.**)* cannot stand alone to make a complete thought in a sentence, but needs an *object*. The action of the transitive verb is "in transit" from the *subject* of the sentence to the *object* or *receiver*. The *transitive verb* falls under SUBJECT + ACTION VERB + OBJECT or S + AV + O pattern. Some verbs are always <u>transitive</u>, like *recognize* in the clause *Eden recognized…* in which the clause is not a complete idea. A noun phrase following the verb tells <u>what</u> or <u>who</u> <u>is needed</u>, as *object* or *completer*.

○ Transitive V, regular, –ed form, past time = **recognized**, with object = *voice*

◊ <u>Eden</u> **/ recognized** *her mother's voice in the dark.* [S + V + O]
    ↑S   ↑AV   ↑O
SN, singular   Object (N phrase completer = *her mother's voice in the dark*)

AV, v. t., –ed form, past time, = **recognized** (V base form = *recognize*)

○ Some verbs may be either *intransitive* or *transitive*, like **teach**.

○ Intransitive V, irregular, **-s** form, present time = **teaches** (V base form = *teach*) ; sentence pattern SN + AV (The complete sentence states that Miss Gonzales is a teacher.)

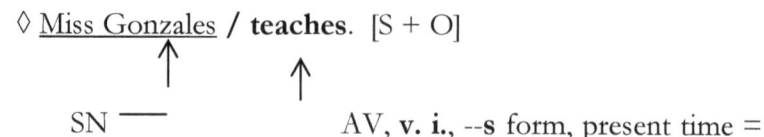

◊ <u>Miss Gonzales</u> **/ teaches.** [S + O]
      ↑   ↑

    SN —   AV, v. i., --s form, present time = **teaches**, agreeing with

                        singular SN = <u>Miss Gonzales</u>, (who is a teacher)

○ Transitive V, irregular, --s form, present time = **teaches** (V base form = *teach*); SN + AV+ DO

            ◊ <u>Miss Gonzales</u> **/ teaches** *Filipino* [S + V + O]
              ↑   ↑   ↑
         SN   O (Object or receiver of the action = *Filipino*)

                      AV, v. t., --s form, present time = **teaches**, agreeing with singular

                      SN = Miss <u>Gonzales</u>, (a teacher in *Filipino*)

(The object (O) *Filipino* is the receiver of the "action" of the verb **teaches**, which is considered "in transit.)

○ Transitive V, regular, **base** form, present time = **dislike**, with object = *advisers*

◊ The <u>citizens</u> **/ dislike** the *advisers* of the President. [S + V + O]
           ↑   ↑   ↑
   SN, plural   Object (N phrase

completer= the *advisers* of the President)

                      AV, regular, **v. t., base** form, present time = **dislike**, agreeing with citizens plural SN = <u>citizens</u>

- *Active and Passive Voices of the Verb.* – *Voice* is a property of the verb *to change in form* that shows whether the *subject* of *the sentence is doing the action* or *is being acted upon.*
  - In *active* sentences, the *subject* or *doer of the action comes first.* The sentence pattern is S + V + O.
  ◊ *Active* = Carla / **rang** the bell.   [sentence pattern = S + V + O]

  SN Carla = *doer of action*   Object
                       AV, past time, *active voice* = **rang** (V base form = *ring*)

  ◊ Active = The batter / **hit** a homerun.

  SN batter = *doer of action*   Object
                       AV, past time, *active voice* = **hit** (V base form = *hit*)

  - In a *passive* sentence, the *subject* is *not the doer* of the action, but *is acted upon;* the *doer* is either *placed at the end* of the sentence, usually after the preposition "by," or *unnamed.*

  ◊ Passive = A homerun / **was hit** *by* the batter. [sentence pattern = S + V]
         SN, singular   HV   MV, past time = **hit** (*past time* AV phrase, *passive* = **was hit**)

  - *Short Passive* = SN *does not perform* the action but *is acted upon* by an unnamed doer

  ◊ Passive = A homerun / **was hit**.
         SN, singular   HV   MV, past time = **hit** (*past time* AV phrase, *passive* = **was hit**)

□ Seven Patterns of Sentences In the English Language
- The subjects, verbs and complements are arranged in seven sentence patterns.

• 1. Sentence Pattern One: SUBJECT + VERB (S + V or S + AV) = The "bare minimum" sentence having no complement or completer or with or without noun marker (determiner or predeterminer). The verb used in Pattern One is intransitive; there is no need of a receiver of the action.

(1) <u>Workers</u> / **strike**.   [Somebody acts.]
     ↑   ↑
  SN   AV

(2) <u>Power</u> / **corrupts**.   [Somethig exists.}
    ↑   ↑
  SN   AV

    (3) <u>Towns</u> / **grow**.   [Something happens.]
         ↑   ↑
    SN   AV

        (4) *The* <u>neighbor</u> / **knocked**.   [Somebody acted.]
             ↑   ↑
        SN   AV   (noun marker = *The*)

                      (5) *A* taxpayer / **had complained**.
        ↑   ↑   ↑
      SN   HV   MV (AV phrase, past perfect time = **had complained**)

• 2. Sentence Pattern Two: SUBJECT + VERB + OBJECT (S + V + O or S + AV + DO) – The sentence in Pattern Two has a complement - the object or target (O). The verb used in Pattern Two is *transitive*, which means that it *carries* the *action across* to the *object* (receiver).

              (1) <u>Dogs</u> / **chase** *cats*.
      SN   AV   DO (receiver of the action = **chase**)

           (2) <u>Filipinos</u> / **like** *mangoes*.
     ↑   ↑   ↑
   SN   AV   DO

• 3.Sentence Pattern Three: SUBJECT + LINKING VERB + PREDICATE NOUN (S + LV + PN) – The verb in Sentence Pattern Three is not an action verb but simply states the condition or being of subject.

                    ◊ The <u>attempt</u> \ **was** a *failure*.
        ↑   ↑   ↑
     SN   LV   PN (*completer* or *complement*)

◊ Cecille Louise \ **became** a *doctor* of medicine.
SN   LV   PN

- 4. Sentence Pattern Four: SUBJECT + LINKING VERB + PREDICATE ADJECTIVE (S + LV + PAdj) Pattern Four is similar to Pattern Three, however, it has a predicate adjective, not a noun, as its completer.

◊ The house \ **is** *green*.   ◊ His venture \ **was** *successful*.
  SN   LV   PAdj   SN   LV   PAdj

- 5. Sentence Pattern Five: SUBJECT + ACTION VERB + INDIRECT OBJECT + DIRECT OBJECT (S + AV + IO + DO) — Pattern Five uses transitive action verb in which the original object (DO) as in the S + AV + DO pattern is passed from one person to another (i. e., postcards are sent from tourists to their families.)

◊ Tourists / **send** their families *postcards*.
SN   AV   IO   DO   (Note: S + V + DO: Tourists / **send** *postcards*.)

◊ The loving daughter / **purchased** her mother a classy sports *car*.
           SN   AV   IO   DO
(**purchased** *car*)

- 6. Sentence Pattern Six: SUBJECT + ACTION VERB + DIRECT OBJECT + OBJECTIVE COMPLEMENT (S + AV + DO + OC) — Objective complement (OC) pins a label on the first object (DO).

◊ My friends / **deemed** the *sale* a tremendous success.
   SN   AV   DO   OC

◊ The manager / **called** *Paul* a genius.
    SN   AV   DO   OC

- 7. Sentence Pattern Seven: SUBJECT + ACTION VERB + DIRECT OBJECT + PREDICATE ADJECTIVE (S + AV + DO + PAdj) — The direct object appears after the verb; the adjective points out the quality of the object. (Although it would seem that the predicate adjective functions like an adverb modifying the verb, this predicate adjective, like the objective complement (OC), pins a label of quality on the object.)

◊ The <u>committee</u> / **considered** the *proposition* foolish.
        ↑   ↑   ↑   ↑
      SN   AV   DO   PAdj (Predicate adjective)

◊ <u>General Miado</u> / **keeps** his *men* alert.
     SN   AV↑   DO↑   PAdj↑

☐ Patterns of Transformation of Sentences

● 1. Transformation One: *Statement* to *Order / Command* – (Declarative To Imperative Sentence)

1) Sentence Pattern One = S + AV to (S + AV) (The subject is not included.)

(Declarative)   (Imperative)

◊ <u>Lucy</u> / **sings.**   ◊ **Sing.**   ◊ (You) / **Sing.**
    ↑   ↑   ↑   ↑
  SN AV AV (SPron) AV

2) Sentence Pattern Two = S + AV + DO

                                  ◊ <u>Felisa</u> / **closed** the *door*. ◊
Close the *door*. ↑   ↑   ↑   ↑   ↑
             SN   AV   DO   AV   DO

3) Sentence Pattern Three = S + LV + N

                                 ◊ <u>Caridad</u> \ **was** my *guest*. ◊
Be my *guest*. ↑   ↑   ↑   ↑   ↑
          SN   LV   N   LV   N

4) Sentence Pattern Four = S + LV + Adj

◊ The <u>children</u> \ **were** *quiet*.   ◊ **Be** *quiet*.   ◊ **Be** *quiet*, children.
            ↑   ↑   ↑   ↑ ↑   ↑ ↑   ↑
           SN   LV   Adj   LV   Adj LV   Adj
(nominative of address=children)

5) Sentence Pattern Five = S + AV + IO + DO

Give Johnny a *medal*. ◊ Noel / **gave** Johnny a *medal*. ◊

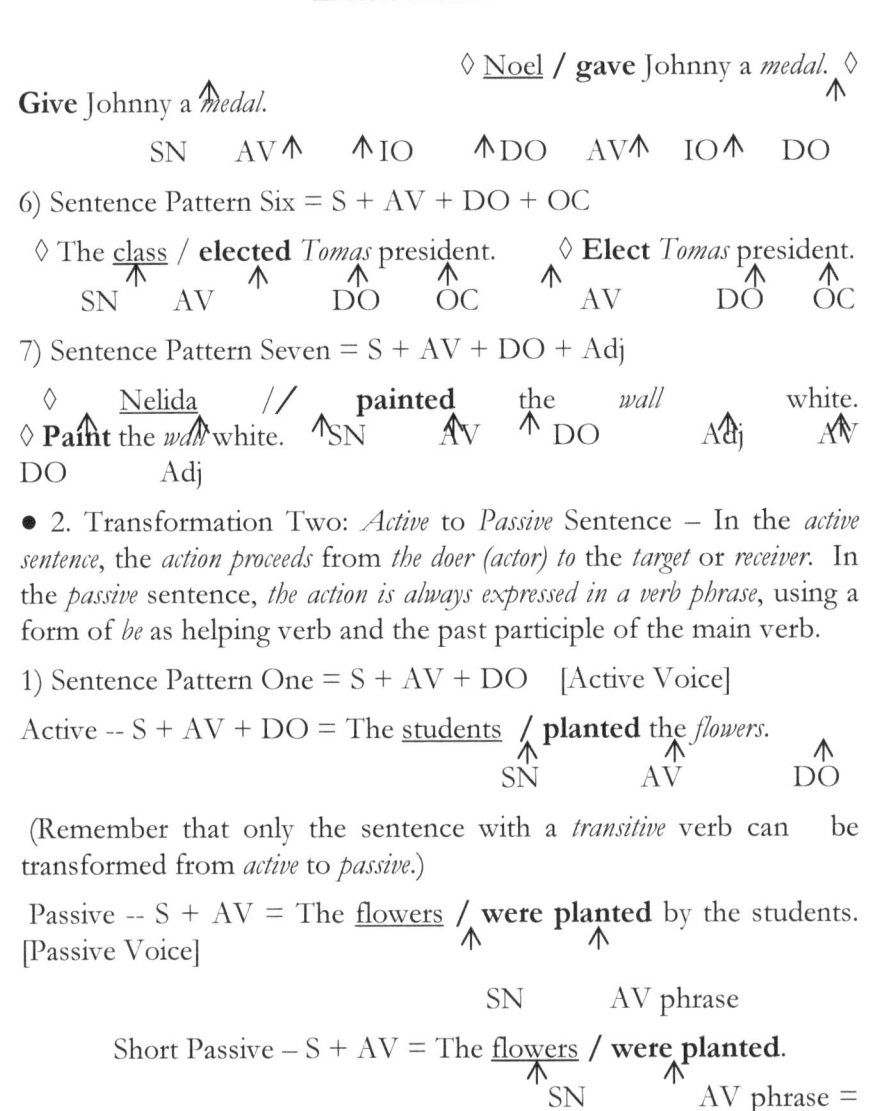

SN AV IO DO   AV IO DO

6) Sentence Pattern Six = S + AV + DO + OC

◊ The class / **elected** *Tomas* president.   ◊ **Elect** *Tomas* president.
SN   AV   DO   OC   AV   DO   OC

7) Sentence Pattern Seven = S + AV + DO + Adj

◊ Nelida // **painted** the *wall* white.
◊ **Paint** the *wall* white.   SN   AV   DO   Adj   AV
DO   Adj

- 2. Transformation Two: *Active* to *Passive* Sentence – In the *active sentence*, the *action proceeds* from *the doer (actor) to* the *target* or *receiver*. In the *passive* sentence, *the action is always expressed in a verb phrase*, using a form of *be* as helping verb and the past participle of the main verb.

1) Sentence Pattern One = S + AV + DO   [Active Voice]

Active -- S + AV + DO = The students / **planted** the *flowers*.
SN   AV   DO

(Remember that only the sentence with a *transitive* verb can be transformed from *active* to *passive*.)

Passive -- S + AV = The flowers / **were planted** by the students. [Passive Voice]

SN   AV phrase

Short Passive – S + AV = The flowers / **were planted**.
SN   AV phrase =
were planted

○The direct object (DO) of the sentence becomes the subject in the passive sentence. The doer in the active sentence seems to appear to be the object, but this is not correct, because the verb is intransitive in the passive sentence. The prepositional phrase *by the students* provides additional idea (who did the planting), but it may be removed as it is not essential to the idea of the passive sentence.

2) Sentence Pattern Six = S + AV + DO + OC

Active : The press / called him a *wizard*.
SN   AV   DO   OC

Passive : He / was called a *wizard* (by the pres
SPron   AV phrase   OC

○ Note that In the passive verb phrase consisting of a form of the verb *be* and the *past participle* of the imain verb (**was called**), **was** may be considered linking verb and **called** adjective. As the verb phrase **was called** has the property or nature of a linking verb, *wizard* may be referred to as objective complement (OC).

• Transformation Three: *Declarative to Interrogative* Sentence – (Raising one's voice at the end to a higher pitch turns a statement into a question.)

◊ Hermie \ is ill. [Statement]

Hermie is ill? [Question]

1) Putting the verb in front of the subject if the verb is only one word

◊   Hermie   \   is   ill.

◊ **Is** Hermie ill?

SN   LV   PAdj   LV   SN   PAdj

2) Switching the auxiliary or helping verb so that it precedes the subject (the first auxiliary

in case of more than one verb phrases)

◊ The mail / has come. ◊ Has the mail come?

SN   HV   MV   HV   SN   MV

3) Placing auxiliary *do* in front of the subject

◊ Franco / works *in a hotel*.   ◊ **Does** Franco work *in a hotel?*

SN AV Adv (Prep phrase)   HV SN MV Adv = *in a hotel*

4) Using *where, when, why* and *how* in questions

◊ The fair / will be held.
◊ Where will the fair be held?
SN   HV HV   MV   Adv   HV   SN HV MV
◊ When will the fair be held?
Adv   HV   SN HV MV
◊ Why will the fair be held?
Adv HV   SN HV MV
◊ How will the fair be held?
Adv HV   SN HV MV

5) Affirmative questions using *do*
◊ Teenagers / need exercise.
◊ Do teenagers need exercise?
SN   AV   O   HV   SN   MV   O

6) Negative question using *do*
◊   Teenagers   /   do   not   **need**   exercise.
◊ **Don't** teenagers need exercise?
          SN   HV Adv MV   O   HV   SN   MV
O   (**Don't** is HV with Adv *not* as a part of it as contracted.)

- Transformation Four: *There is* sentences – The expletive *there* precedes the verb (form of *be*). *There* is one of the delaying tactics in grammar – meaning to delay the subject when it is needed to carry the main stress.

◊ Students / are practicing in the playground.
   SN   HV   MV

◊ *There* are students practicing in the playground. (expletive *there* delays the subject)
       HV   SN   MV

o The "cleft" sentence allows any element in the sentence to carry the main stress by using the "generalized" *it*.

(1) In 1990 a strong typhoon caused great damage.

It was in <u>1990</u> when a strong typhoon caused great damage.

It was a strong <u>typhoon</u> that caused great damage.

It was a great <u>damage</u> that was caused by a strong typhoon.

○ Another cleft transformation that *changes* the *stress* makes use of *what*

(1) The PIRMA movement of gathering signatures to amend the Constitution exasperated the people.

What exasperated the people is the PIRMA movement of gathering signatures to amend the Constitution.

☐ Phrases

• A phrase is a group of related words without a subject or a verb or both. A phrase can never be a sentence.

◊ *Huge, fierce* and *hungry* = Adjective participial phrase modifying <u>lion</u>

  Huge, fierce and *hungry,* the <u>lion</u> / **charged** against its prey.

            SN AV

◊ *Looming huge, fierce and hungry,* the <u>lion</u> / **charged** *in the most best manner.*

 (Participial phrase Adj), SN AV Adv = *in the most bestial manner,* modifying SN = <u>lion</u>

(A*dverbial prep phrase*)

• Kinds of Phrases – Single or one-word adjectives and adverbs "color" or add details of specificity to writing precision and give ideas variety, vigor and straightforwardness. Phrases help do the trick to attain clarity and precision in writing with a style. The three kinds of common phrases are 1) prepositional phrase, 2) appositive phrases and 3) verbal phrases. The first two phrases are used only as modifiers, while the verbal phrase may serve both as the subject and modifier in a sentence.

•1) Prepositional Phrase – A preposition used together with other parts of speech may function as *adjective* (prepositional adjectival phrase) or *adverb* (*prepositional adverbial phrase*).

○ *Prepositional phrase* as *adjective*

◊ The girl *with long hair* \ **is** this year's class valedictorian.
SN   Prep phrase, Adj (Which girl? = *with long hair*, modifying SN = girl)

◊ Rodelyn / **works** as manager *of Riverside Café*.
   SN   AV   PN   Prep phrase, Adj = *of Riverside Café*, modifying PN = manager

◊ The flowers *in the corner* / **came** *from Lita's garden.*

   SN   AV   Adv, prep phrase = *from Lita's garden*,
                                    modifying AV = **came**
            Adj Prep phrase = *in the corner*, modifying SN = flowers

◊ The President / **traveled** *around the world* to attract investors *in the heavy industries.*
   SN   AV
        Adv = *around the world*,   Adj = *in the heavy industries*,
        modifying AV = **traveled**   modifying N = investors

○ *Prepositional phrase* as *adverb*

◊ The scientist / **traveled** *by foot* alone.

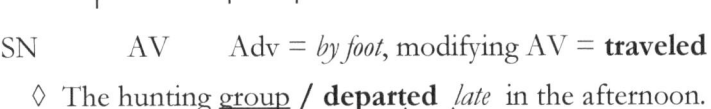

    SN   AV   Adv = *by foot*, modifying AV = **traveled**

◊ The hunting group / **departed** *late* in the afternoon.
                       AV

Adv = *late* modifying AV = **departed**   Adv = *in the afternoon*, modifying Adv = *late*)

□ Exercise 18 : On your paper, write down and identify the *prepositional phrase* in each sentence as *adjective* or *adverb*.

1. The Cruzes built a big house of bamboos between two tall acacia trees.
2. He bought his car from a dealer store on Mabini Street.
3. The chief of the police station launched the manhunt without delay.
4. Children dug the sand on the beach for turtle eggs.
5. Felino fired his gun into the air to scare the goons.
6. The jet aircraft flew into the clouds towards east.
7. Mathilde rubbed the powder puff on her face with a smile.
8. From his vantage point, Fernando observed her on the swing.
9. Perfecto climbed the roof of the store in fear of the intimidating dog.
10. The owner of the house accommodated a guest from Manila.

• 2) Appositive and Appositive Phrases – An appositive is a noun or pronoun placed near another noun or pronoun to explain, rename or identify it.

◊ Miss Armi Kuusela, *the Miss Universe from Finland,* / **married** *a Filipino* Mr. Virgilio

Hilario. [Appositive phrase = *The Miss Universe from Finland* renaming Miss Armi

Kuusela; appositive phrase = *a Filipino* identifying the nationality of Mr. Virgilio

Hilario.]

o An essential appositive phrase is necessary to the meaning of the sentence. In the example, *Mr. Virgilio Hilario* is the appositive of *a Filipino* and is not set off by a comma.

o A nonessential appositive phrase is not necessary to the meaning of the sentence, and this appositive is set off from the rest of the sentence by a comma. The *Miss Universe from Finland* is the appositive of *Miss*

Armi Kuusela and is set off by a comma because it is not necessary to the meaning of the sentence.

o An appositive may precede the word that it renames or modifies.

◊ *A frightening experience*, his <u>fall</u> from a high rise building \ **will remain** etched in his memory. (Appositive phrase: *a frightening experience* renames subject *fall*)

◊ The <u>*superintendent* Mr. Ramon Roxas</u> \ **was** consistent in his decisions.

□ Exercise 20 : Write the appositive phrases and identify whether nonessential or essential.

1. The CPU cultural group Tumandok received a warm welcome.

2. Eliseo, the good farmer, always voted in the past elections.

3. Senator Gloria Arroyo, the vice presidentiable, was our guest speaker.

4. Land Bank, a countryside development bank, lends money to the farmers.

   (Appositives may be used in various ways.)

1. The car, a BMW racer, sideswiped a gorgeous woman.

2. Renato painted a rustic landscape, a scenic mountain paradise.

3. The philanthropist donated one million pesos to his Alma Mater, the Don Casimero Andrada National High School.

□ Clauses

- A clause is a group of words having both a subject (noun phrase) and a predicate (verb phrase) and *may* or *may not express* a complete thought or idea. When a clause conveys a complete idea, it is a sentence and is also referred to as an 1) independent clause. It is a 2) dependent or subordinate clause when it does not express a complete thought.

o 1) Independent or main clause – It is a sentence, being a group of words that expresses a complete thought. *Two independent clauses*:

◊ Ten members of the Arroyo Cabinet / tendered their resignation; the others / stayed put.

o 2) Dependent or subordinate clause – This group of words acts as *adverbial modifier* in a

complex sentence.

◊ The <u>Moro National Liberation Front</u> / **signed** a peace agreement with the government,

  because they / wanted peace and progress.

The sentence is also called complex that shows cause and effect relationship. The *dependent clause modifying the main clause* is an adverbial clause. The dependent clause *because they wanted peace and progress* shows the reason for the agreement.

• Kinds of subordinate clauses according to use or function

o 1) Adverbial clause – It is a modifier of the action in a complex sentence. The adverbial clause introduced by the adverb *when*.

  ◊ <u>Filipinos</u> / **manifest** their resiliency *when adversity strikes.*

o 2) Adjective (adjectival) clause – It is a modifier of the SN introduced by the relative pronoun *who which* or *that.*

◊ The <u>soldier</u> *who merited the Medal of Valor* / **led** the unsuccessful mutiny.

o 3) Noun clause – It is introduced by *that* and is used as (1) subject, (2) direct object of the verb, (3) predicate noun, (4) appositive and (5) object of a preposition. (The clauses are *italicized*.)

◊ *Subject* = <u>That she is sincere in her desire to help</u> / **was appreciated** by the victims.

◊ *Object of the verb* = Most <u>people</u> / **agree** *that he deserved his comeuppance.*

  ◊ *Predicate nominative* = Paolo's <u>problem</u> \ **is** *that his marks are on* a downhill.

  ◊ *Appositive* = Her <u>suggestion</u> *that they spend a week in Boracay* / **was rejected**.

◊ *Object of a preposition* = The <u>group</u> / **had** no idea *on where to get the funds.*

◘ Some Salient Points on The Changes in the Forms of Verbs (See Tabulated List of Verb Forms at end of this guide.)

☐ 1. The *Simple Present Time* (The Simple Present Tense) – Verb agreeing with *Plural Noun*

• The Simple Present Time expressed by the Base Form of the Verb – The *base form* of the verb is also called the *root verb*. It is the base form or root verb that appears first or is listed first in the dictionary; it is used to look up a verb for its meaning.

• The *base form expresses* the *simple present time* of the *regular* or *irregular verb as used* in a sentence for plural (1) *subject noun* (SN), 2) plural *subject pronoun* (SPron) or 3) the *subject pronoun* (SPron) is You, or I.

○ 1) AV, regular, *simple present* time, *base form* = **fish**, for plural SN = men

◊ Men / fish.
　　　↑　　　↑
　SN, plural　　AV, regular, base form, simple present time = **fish**, agreeing with plural SN = men

○ 2) AV, irregular, *simple present* time, *base form* = **teach**, for pronoun they

◊ They / teach.
　SPron,↑　　↑ AV, irregular, base form, simple present time = **teach**, agreeing with

　　plural　　　SPron, plural = they

○ 3) AV, irregular, *simple present* time, **base** form = **sing**, for pronoun you

◊ You / sing songs that tell us of your cultural heritage.　　(I / sing songs…)
　　SPron↑　　↑　　AV, base form, simple present time = **sing**, agreeing with SPron = you *

○ LV, present time = **am**, used with pronoun I only

◊ I \ **am** a teacher.
　SPron,↑　↑ LV, present time = **am** (SOBV = *be*), agreeing only with SPron = I

□ 1b. The *Simple Present Time* (The Simple Present Tense) – Verb agreeing with *Singular Noun*

• 1b) The Simple Present Time of the verb expressed by the –S form of the verb – The *simple present time* of the verb is expressed by the --s form when the subject is singular.

• The –s form is done by **adding** –*s* to the **base** form of the regular verb **ending** in 1) a **consonant,** 2) **vowel *e*** and 3) *y*, **preceded by a vowel.** The *suffix* –**es** is added to the **base** form of the verbs **ending** in 3a) *y*, **preceded by** a **consonant, after changing y** to *i*, 4) **ch, sh** and 5) **o, oo.**

○ 1) AV, base form, regular, *ending in* a **consonant** = **talk** is changed to --**s** form, *simple present time* by adding –s = **talks**, for singular SN = Riza

◊ Riza / talks.
　　↑　　　↑
　　SN,　　AV, --s form, simple present time = **talks** (V base form = *talk*),
　　singular　　agreeing with singular SN = Riza

○ 2) AV, base form, regular, *ending in* **e** = **console** is changed to --**s** form, *simple present time* by adding –s = **consoles**, for singular SN = Fe

◊ Fely / consoles her grief-stricken friend.
　　↑　　　↑
SN, singular　　AV, --s form, simple present time = **consoles** (V base form = *console*), agreeing with singular SN = Fely

○ 3) AV, base form, regular, *ending* in a *vowel-preceded* **y** = **prey**, changed to --**s** form, *simple present time* by adding –s = **preys**, for singular SN = eagle

◊ The eagle / **preys** on rodents and other small animals.
　　SN, singular↑　　↑AV, regular, --s form, simple present time = **preys** (V base form = *prey*), agreeing with singular SN = eagle

○ 3a) AV, base form, regular, *ending* in a *consonant-preceded* y = **beautify** is changed to --**s** form, *simple present time* by *adding* –**es**, *after changing* y *to* **i** = **beautifies**, for singular SN = Kim

◊ Kim / **beautifies** the school landscape with flowering plants.
　　↑　　↑

SN, singular   AV, --s form, simple present time = **beautifies**
(V base form = *beautify*),

agreeing with singular SN = Kim

○ 4) AV, base form, regular, *ending in* **ch** = **watch** is changed to **--s** form, *simple present time* by *adding* **–es** = **watches,** for singular SN = dog

◊ The loyal dog / **watches** over its master's grave.
              ↑   ↑

          SN, singular   AV, regular, **--s** form, simple present time = **watches** (V base

form = watch), agreeing with singular SN = dog

○ 4a) AV, base form, regular, *ending in* **sh** = **rush** is changed to **--s** form, *simple present time* by *adding* **–es** = **rushes,** for singular SN = Pen

◊ Pen / **rushes** to deliver the mail.
       ↑   ↑

   SN, singular   AV, **--s** form, simple present time = **rushes**
(V base form = *rush*), agreeing with singular SN = Pen

○ 5) AV, base form, regular, *ending in* **o** = **zero** is changed to **--s** form, *simple present time* by adding **–es** = **zeroes**, for singular SN = pilot

◊ The pilot / **zeroes** in on the target before making the dive.
              ↑   ↑

   SN, singular   AV, **--s** form, simple present time = **zeroes**
(V base form = *zero*),

agreeing with singular SN = pilot

○ 5a) AV, base form, regular, *ending in* **oo** = **moo** is changed to **--s** form, *simple present time* by *adding* **–es** = **mooes**, for singular SN = cow

◊ The cow / **mooes** to call her calf.
            ↑   ↑

SN, singular   AV, --s form, simple present time = **mooes** (V base form = *moo*),

agreeing with singular SN = cow

- *Irregular verbs.* The *irregular verb* that expresses the *present time* is changed to the *–s form* when the *subject* is *singular*; *irregular verbs* 1) **catch** and 1a) **teach** are *changed* to *–s* form, by *adding* **–es** to the **base** form. In the case of 2) **fly**, like the *consonant-preceded y-*ending regular verbs, *y* *is changed to i before adding* the *suffix* **--es**.

  ○ 1) AV, base form, irregular, *ending in* **ch** = **catch**, changed to --s form, *simple present time* by *adding* **–es** = **catches**, for singular SN = Dindo

  ◊ Dindo / **catches** frogs for sale to food gourmands.

  SN, singular   AV, irregular, --s form, simple present time = **catches** (V base form =

  catch), agreeing with singular SN = Dindo

  ○ 1a) AV, base form, irregular, *ending in* **ch** = **teach** is changed to **–s** **form**, *simple present time* by *adding* **–es** = **teaches**, for singular SN = Remy

  ◊ Remy / **teaches** Science and Technology at Lambunao National High School.

  SN, singular   AV, irregular, --s form, simple present time = **teaches** (V base form =

  teach), agreeing with singular SN = Remy

  ○ 2) AV, base form, irregular, ending in **y** *preceded by* a **consonant** = **fly** is changed to **--s** *form, simple present time* by *add ing* **–es**, *after changing* **y** to **i**= **flies**, for singular SPron = it

  ◊ It / **flies** like a bird.

  SPron,   AV, irregular, --s form, simple present time = **flies** (V base form = *fly*), singular   (**y** is to changed to **i** & **--es** added), agreeing with singular SPron = It

☐ 2. The *Future Time* of the *Verb* (Future Tense)

● The *simple future time indicated* by *modals*. – A verb expresses a future time, aside from the present and the past times. There is *no specific verb form for the future time*; *modals* are used together with the *base form* of the verb to show futurity. Modals (MHV) **will** and **shall**, *as well as the other modals,* signify future time. (The *future time* of the verb *is studied ahead* of the *past time,* as *the present time* of the verb with the use of appropriate modifier can show futurity.)

◊ Fran / will sing in the program.

            MV, **base** form, simple present time = **sing**

            HVM = **will** (MHV = *modal*), signifying future time

          >AV phrase, *simple future time* = **will sing**

● *Futurity* or *future time may be signified by* an *adverb* of *time* used together with the present form of the verb, **base** or **–s form.**

○ AV, base form, simple present time = **go** ; Adv of time = *on Sunday,* showing a ***future time***

◊ Ike, Nido and Sam / go to Bacolod *on Sunday.*

| AV, **base** form, SN, Sunday, modifying AV = plural, compound noun) **go,** signifying *future time* | Adv, (Prep phrase) = *on* present time = **go**, agreeing with plural SN = Ike, Nido and Sam |

○ AV, **--s** form, simple present time = **meets** ; Adv of time = *tomorrow,* modifying AV = **meets**, expressing a ***future time***

◊ The coach / **meets** the team at the airport *tomorrow.*

           ↑   ↑

SN, singular   AV, --s form, present time ——————— Adv
= *tomorrow*, modifying

                          = **meets** (V base form = *meet*),   AV
= **meets**, signifying

                          agreeing with singular SN = <u>coach</u>
future time

• The '***three times***' in ***a simple present time verb*** reflecting habitual action = **base** form or **–s** form verb, *without any adverbial modifier*, like **sing**, or **loves**, etc., can imply the *past, present* and *future times*.

  ○ AV, base form, simple present time = **sing**, *implying* the ***past, present*** and ***future times***, as shown

       ◊ <u>They</u> / **sing** songs of praise.

          ↑   ↑

    SPron, plural   AV, **base** form, present time = **sing**, agreeing, with plural SPron = <u>they</u>

Past = <u>They</u> / **sang** in the *past*.

Present = <u>They</u> / **sing** at *present*.

    Future = <u>They</u> / **will sing** in the *future as long as they are able to*.

  ○ AV, **–s** form, simple present time = **loves,** *encompassing* the ***past, present*** and ***future*** times.

       ◊ <u>Ophelia</u> / **loves** her children.
         ↑   ↑

    SN, singular   AV, **–s** form = **loves** (V base form = *love*), agreeing with singular

                 SN = <u>Ophelia</u>

    Past = <u>Ophelia,</u> *a*s a mother, / **loved** her children since they were born.

    Present = <u>She</u> / **loves** them now.

    Future = <u>She</u> / **will love** them as long as she is able to.

○ LV, present time = **is**, reflecting *generally accepted idea* in the ***past, present*** and ***future times***

◊ Milk \ **is** good for everybody.
　　↑　↑
SN, singular　　LV, present time = **is** (SOBV = *be*)

Past = Milk, as nutritious food, \ **was** good for everybody then.

Present = Milk \ **is** good for everybody now.

Future = Milk \ **will be** good for everybody in the future.

● *The base form or –s form* of the verb, like (1) **attend,** or (2) **live,** along with an adverb showing *habitual action,* may also express the *three times* of the verb.

◊ (1) The children / **attend** classes *every day*.

　　　SN, plural ↑　　↑　Adverbial phrase = *every day* (two-words), modifying

　　AV = **attend,** showing habitual action

　　AV, base form = **attend,** agreeing with plural SN = children

Past = The children / **attended** classes after enrolment.

Present = The children / **attend** classes at present.

Future = The children / **will continue** attending classes every day until they graduate.

　　◊ (2) Federico / **lives** in Lambunao.
　　　　↑　↑
　　SN, singular　　　　AV, regular, **--s** form, present time = **lives** (V base form = *live*)

Past = Federico / **lived** in Lambunao since birth.

Present = Federico / **lives** in Lambunao now.

　　Future = Federico / **will live** in Lambunao in the *future as long as he is living.*

.□ 3. The *Simple Past Time* or *–ed Form* for *Regular Verbs* (The Simple Past Tense)

• The simple past time or the –ed form. – The *simple past time* of the *regular verb* is the *–ed form for plural* or *singular subject*. The **regular verb** is changed from the *present form* (**base form**) to the *past form* or **–ed form** in a regular pattern by 1) *adding* suffix **–ed** to the *base form* of the regular verb *ending* in a **consonant**, including 1a) **y** preceded by a vowel or 2) suffix **–d** to the verb ending in **e**. Regular verbs that end in *consonants* are changed to the **–ed** forms by 3) *doubling* the *last letters before adding* the suffix **--ed**. However, when the consonant is preceded by a *double vowel* as in verbs like **brief, dread, fool, peel**, etc., the suffix **--ed** is 4) *added without doubling* the *last letter*.

○ 1) AV, base form, regular, simple present time, *ending in a* **consonant** = **help** ; **--ed** added to the base form = **helped**, –ed form, *simple past time*

◊ The policeman / **helped** us cross the street yesterday.
　　　　↑　　　　　　↑
　　SN, singular　　　AV, regular, **--ed** form, simple past time = **helped** (V base form = *help*)

○1a) AV, base form, regular, simple present time, *ending in* **y** preceded by a *vowel* = **play** ;

--ed added to the base form = **played**, **–ed** form, *simple past time*

◊ The men / **played** Scrabble.
　　↑　　　↑
　　SN, plural　　AV, regular, **--ed** form, simple past time = **played** (V base form = *play*)

○(2) AV, base form, regular, simple present time, *ending in* **vowel** e = **participate** ; only **–d** added to the base form = **participated**, **--ed** form, *simple past time*

◊ The girls / **participated** in the parade last Monday.
　　↑　　　　↑

SN, plural   AV, regular, --**ed** form, simple past time = **participated** (V base form

= *participate*); [Note: **participate** always needs the Prep = *in*) = The parade was *participated in* by the natives of the barangay.]

o 3) AV, base form, regular, simple present time, ending in a **consonant** = **abet** ; *consonant doubled* before adding **–ed** to the base form = **abetted**, --ed form, *simple past time*

◊ The <u>guard</u> / **abetted** the commission of the offense by his laxity.   ↑   ↑

SN, singular   AV, regular, --**ed** form, simple past time = **abetted** (V base form =

abet)

o 4) AV, base form, regular, simple present time, ending in a **consonant** *preceded by a double vowel* = **peel** ; *consonant not doubled before adding* –ed *to the base form* = **peeled**, --ed form, *simple past time*

◊ The <u>boys</u> / **peeled** the potatoes in no time at all.
       ↑   ↑

SN, plural   AV, --**ed** form, simple past time = **peeled** (V base form = *peel*)

□ 3a. The *Simple Past Time* or *–ed Form* of *Irregular Verbs* (Simple Past Tense)

• The *past time* or the *–ed form* of *irregular* verb is made by a **change in spelling that does not follow any rule**. It means that the **–en form** for each **irregular verb** has been **provided arbitrarily**, or *as conventionally agreed upon* by grammarians. Hence, the *–ed forms* of the *irregular verbs* must be <u>memorized</u>.

o AV, *irregular,* base form, simple present time = **buy** ; past time, *arbitrarily provided* = **bought**, --**ed** form, simple past time

◊ <u>We</u> / **bought** books in Iloilo City.
    ↑
        ↑

SPron, AV, irregular, --**en** form, simple past time = **bought**
(V base form = *buy*)
plural

☐ Using Multiple Helping Verbs to Make Verb Phrases Express a Variety of Meanings in Sentences

• Aside from *indicating the time of the sentences, auxiliaries* or *helping verbs* make the verb phrases *express* a *variety of meanings*. The *three simple times* of the verbs are presented in order to appreciate the changes in meanings in the sentences using helping or auxiliary verbs.

○ The *Simple Present Time* AV, *showing present action* ; regular, **--s** form, *active voice* = **washes**, for singular subject / (**wash**, for plural subject)

◊ Bert / **washes** the car.
SN, singular ↑   ↑ AV, **--s** form, simple present time, *active voice* = **washes** (V base form =

wash), agreeing with singular SN = Bert, and *showing present action*

○ The *Simple Past Time* AV, *showing past action* ; regular, **--ed** form, *active voice* = **washed**, for plural or singular subject

◊ Bert / **washed** the car.
SN,↑   ↑ AV, **--ed** form, simple past time, *active voice* = **washed** (V base form =

singular   *wash*), *showing past action*

○ The *Simple Future Time* AV phrase, *indicating futurity of action and future obligation of someone* ; active voice (**HVM** + **MV**) = **should wash**, for plural or singular subject ; HVM, past form = **should** (**shall** is used if the obligation is a requirement according to law, rules or regulations) ; MV, regular, **base** form = **wash**

◊ Bert / **should wash** the car.
SN, ↑   ↑   ↑ MV, **base** form, present time= **wash**

singular   HVM, past form of *shall* = **should** (HV = *modal*), *indicating futurity*

○ 1) The *Present Time* AV phrase, *indicating action in the present ; passive voice* (**HV + MV**) = **is washed**, for singular subject / (**are washed**, for plural subject) ; HV, present time, be = **is** ; MV, **--ed** form, past participle = **washed** (V base form = *wash*)

◊ The car / is washed by Bert.

SN, singular ⬆ ⬆   ⬆ MV, **--ed** form, past participle = **washed**
(V base form = *wash*)

HV, present time = **is** (HV = *be*), agreeing with singular SN = car

○ 2) The *Past Time* AV phrase, *showing past action ; passive voice* (**HV + MV**) = **was washed**, for singular subject / (**were washed**, for plural subject) ; HV, past time, be = **was** ; MV, regular, **--ed** form, past participle = **washed**

◊ The car / was washed by Bert.

⬆   ⬆   ⬆
SN, singular   MV, **--ed** form, past participle = **washed**
(V base form = *wash*)

HV, present time = **was** (HV = *be*), agreeing with singular SN = car

○ 3) The *Future Time* AV phrase, *indicating future action ; passive voice* (**HVM HV + MV**) = **will be washed**, for plural or singular subject ; HVM, present form = **will** ; MHV, present time = **be** ; MV, regular, **--ed** form, past participle = **washed**

◊ The car / will be washed by Bert.
    ⬆   ⬆ ⬆ ⬆

SN, singular   MV, **--ed** form, past participle = **washed** (V base form =*wash*)

MHV, present time = **be** (HV = *be*)

HVM, present form = **will** (HV = *modal*)

○ 4) The *Present Progressive Time* AV phrase, *showing work being done at present ; active voice* (**HV + MV**) = **is washing**, for singular subject / (**are washing**, for plural subject) ; HV, present time, be = **is** ; MV, regular, **--ing** form, present participle = **washing**

◊ <u>Bert</u> / **is washing** the car.
　　↑　　　　↑
　　　　　↑

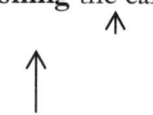

SN,　　　　　MV, regular, --**ing** form, present participle = **washing** (V base form =

singular　　　*wash*)

HV, present time = **is** (HV = *be*), agreeing with singular SN = <u>Bert</u>

○ 5) The *Past Progressive Time* **AV** phrase, *showing action being done at a time in the past* ; active voice (**HV** + **MV**) = **was washing**, for <u>singular</u> subject ╱ (**were washing**, for <u>plural</u> subject) ; HV, past time, *be* = **was** ; MV, regular, --**ing** form, present participle = **washing**

◊ <u>Bert</u> / **was washing** the car.
　　↑　　↑　　↑

SN,　　　　　MV, regular, --**ing** form, present participle = **washing** (V base form = *wash*)

HV, past time = **was** (HV = *be*), agreeing with singular SN = <u>Bert</u>

○ 9) The *future progressive time* AV phrase, *expressing probability of someone doing an obligation* ; active voice (**HVM** + **MHV** + **MV**) = **should be washing**, for <u>plural</u> or <u>singular</u> subject ; HVM, past form = **should** ; MHV, present time, *be* ; MV, regular, --**ing** form, present participle = **washing**

◊ <u>Bert</u> / **should be washing** the car.

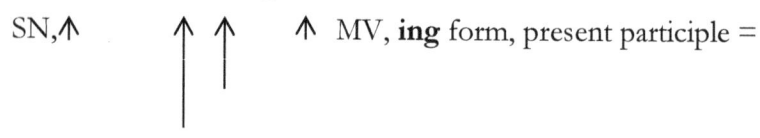

SN,↑　　　↑ ↑　　↑ MV, **ing** form, present participle =
　　　　　　│

washing (V base form = *wash*)

MHV, present time = **be** (HV = *be*)

HVM, future time, (past form of *shall*) = **should**

○ 10) The *Present Perfect Time* **AV** phrase, *showing action completed at the time of speaking* ; *active voice* (**HV** + **MV**) = **has washed**, for singular subject / (**have washed**, for plural subject) ; HV, present time = **has** ; MV, regular, **--ed** form, past participle = **washed**

◊ Bert / **has washed** the car.

    SN, ⋏   ⋏ ⋏ MV, **--ed** form, past participle = **washed** (V base form = *wash*)

              HV, present time = **has** (SOBV = *have*), agreeing with singular SN = Bert

○ 11) The *Past Perfect Time* AV phrase, *showing action completed* ; *active voice* (**HV** + **MV**) = **had washed**, for plural or singular subject ; HV, past time = **had** ; MV, regular, **--ed** form, past participle = **washed**

◊ Bert / **had washed** the car.

    SN, singular   ⋏   ⋏ MV, **--ed** form, past participle = **washed**(V base form = *wash*)

              HV, past time = **had** (SOBV = *have*), agreeing with singular SN = Bert

○ 12) The *Future Perfect Time* **AV** phrase, *expressing failed obligation on the part of someone* ; *active voice* (**HVM** + **MHV** + **MV**) = **should have washed**, for plural or singular subject ; HVM, past form = **should** ; MHV, present time = **have** ; MV, regular, **--ed** form, past participle = **washed**

◊ Bert / **should have washed** the car.
   ⋏   ⋏   ⋏   ⋏

SN, singular   MV, **--ed** form, past participle = **washed** (V base form *wash*)

              MHV, present time = **have** (SOBV = *have*)

HVM, future time, past form of shall) = **should** (SOBV = *modal*)

○ 13) The *present perfect progressive time* AV phrase, showing one probably doing his job at the time of speaking ; *active voice* (**HV + MHV + MV**) = **has been washing**, for singular subject ∕ (**have been washing**, for plural subject) ; HV, present time = **has** ; MHV, --**en** form, be = **been** ; MV, regular, --**ed** form, present participle = **washing**

◊ Bert / **has been washing** the car.

SN, singular ↑ ↑ ↑ MV, --**ing** form, present participle =

washing (V base form = *wash*)

                HV, present time = **has** (SOBV = *have*)

                MHV, --**en** form = **been** (SOBV = *be*)

○ 14) *The Past Perfect Progressive Time* AV *phrase, expressing probability of one doing his job at a given past time* ; *active voice* (**HV + MHV + MV**) = **had been washing**, for plural or singular subject ; HV, past time = **had** ; MHV, --**en** form, *be* = **been** ; MV, regular, --**ing** form = **washing**

    ◊ Bert ∕ **had been washing** the car.

SN, singular↑   ↑   MV, --**ing** form, present participle =
washing (V base form

              ↑   MHV, ↑--**en** form = **been** (SOBV =*be*)
wash)

            HV, past time of *has* = **had** (SOBV = *have*)

○ 15) The *Future Perfect Progressive Time* AV phrase, *showing one ought to do his job* ; *active voice* (**HVM + HV + MHV + MV**) = **should have been washing**, for plural or singular subject ; HVM, past form = **should** ; HV, present time = **have** ; MHV, --**en** form, *be* = **been** ; MV, regular, --**ing** form = **washing**

◊ Bert / **should have been washing** the car.

SN, singular↑   ↑ ↑ ↑ ↑

MV, --**ing** form, present participle = **washing** (V base
 MHV, --**en** form = **been** (SOBV = *be*)   form = *wash*)
 HV, present time = **have** (SOBV = *have*)
 HVM, future time (past form of *shall*) = **should** (SOBV = *modal*)

☐ Exercise 19 : Write on your paper the verb phrases and state the time and voice of each phrase.

1. Ariel lends his bicycle to Owen.
2. Danton served the AFP Medical Corps for thirty years.
3. Lessons in swimming are given to the recruits.
4. Eden had passed the teachers board.
5. Roger's new motorcycle was gone when his brother arrived.
6. Matches for lawn tennis will be written on the bulletin board.
7. Andrea had been reading grammar books.
8. Rupert was building a birdhouse.
9. Irene will be running in the marathon tomorrow.
10. Lambino has left his estate in the care of Joe.
11. Isidra had given a tidy sum of money to Ben.
12. Rebecca will have married Claro at this time.
13. Ann has been singing classical songs all day.
14. Lenida had been tending the pigs until her sister took over.
15. Araceli will have been taking the teacher's test at this time now.
16. Sandino is marrying Arsenie on Monday.
17. Anita likes broiled catfish.
18. Felix has voted to reappoint Oscar janitor.
19. Inocencio did not agree with Salvador on the office procedures to follow.

20. Niel has proven himself as a very responsible family man.

☐ Exercise 20 : Write the verb phrases. Underline the auxiliary or helping verb once and the main verb twice.

1. Crackers will stay crisp if they are kept in a tin box.
2. Nonilo's repair job would have been simple had he used the right tool.
3. Ina was coming down the stairs when she stumbled.
4. Felipe should also observe good neighborly relations.
5. All the boys who need new uniforms should pick them up in the athletic director's office?
6. Storms can be located by satellite.
7. An airport of international standard will soon be built in Sta.Barbara - Cabatuan area.
8. Lauro could have spent his vacation in Boracay.
9. The monkey should have climbed the tree to eat the fruits.
10. Had I taken more time, I could have done better.

☐ Exercise 21 – List down the verbs or verb phrases found in this selection.

Since ancient times, tea has always been the elixir of life, the prime health beverage in countries like Japan, China and Korea. That tea aids in digestion and cleansing, and is an anti-oxidant and an anti-cancer potion has long been confirmed. Research has identified polyphenols as the cancer-fighting ingredients, particularly present in tea.

Coffee was once shunned as a drink that simply keeps you awake and leaves you the jitters. Even British Prime Minister Tony Blair was once advised to drink less coffee.

Now medical researchers are eating humble pie along with cups of coffee. Coffee, they now declare, contains cancer-fighting polyphenols just like green tea.

Dr. Julian Whitaker says coffee has the ability to help treat migraine, Parkinson's disease, colon cancer and asthma as well as liver, kidney and gallstone problems. It also boosts athletic performance by improving the body's ability to release and burn fat from storage.

But how much coffee is good for the body?

"No more than three to four cups daily," says Dr. Chiara Trombetti.

"One and one-fourth cups of coffee a day deliver the benefits of tannin, an anti-oxidant that's good for the heart, good for the liver and prevents cirrhosis. Coffee effectively filters the oils that contribute to the raising of bad cholesterol," Dr. Trombetti explains.

So go ahead and relax in your favorite coffee and tea place. Confucius says, tea is okay. One and one-fourth cups of coffee a day keep the doctor away. – *M.M.M., Phil. Star.*

☐ Exercise 24 : Identify the verb phrases by indicating the time and voice

1. They are glued to the TV watching Pacquiao's fight.

2. The children were mesmerized by the magician.

3. The wind is blowing from east to west which slows down our travel.

4. Isabelo was planning to marry Julieta when we left their barangay.

5. The rat had outwitted the cat, although it was cornered by the latter.

6. We shall see what we can do for the hungry chicks.

7. Ritzy shall improve his class standing or Rica will emerge as valedictorian.

8. Giancarlo is known in the city as a smart detective.

9. Remo shall have washed the rice seedlings for transplanting.

10. The eagled had laid only two eggs.

☐ Exercise 22 : Write on your paper the auxiliary or helping verb and identify the time and the subject noun or pronoun that it agrees with.

1. Lydia has gone to Manila..
2. Urduja was elected as member of the board of directors of their union.
3. Nilo was authorized by the president to lead the five groups of cub scouts.
4. Aurora is bent on pushing for the approval of motion of Jose to postpone the group tour.
5. Katrina has negotiated for the sale of the mansion with all the heirs.
6. Ana's doves have fed themselves on the grains in the drying yard.
7. Gunrunners were unloading some cargo when the police surprised them.
8. Each winning entry will be awarded a certificate of excellence.
9. Rudy was questioning the suspect hogtied to an anthill.
10. Nelio will be enrolling in nursing this semester in deference to his mother.
11. Every able-bodied student is enjoined to participate in the sports fest.
12. Simon should have cancelled the game on account of the heavy downpour.
13. The boys had skipped classes to go to the mall.
14. Omar has been eating pie after pie to the consternation of the cook.
15..Ardee's carabaos have been wallowing in the mud for three hours now.
16. Danny did not pass the test.
17. Lillibeth had been holding classes in the rice field when we arrived at the area.

18. Elsie shall have been painting the porch as requested by her aunt.
19. Rima, Eva and Ester are praying the rosary in the church.
20. Mila is not known in the community.

☐ Adjectives – Adjectives give "color" to nouns and pronouns

• Adjectives (Adj) describe or modify nouns or pronouns by giving "color" to make them more specific. Below are some predicate nouns or PN being "colored" by adjectives. An adjective answers any one of the following questions: 1) *What kind?*, 2) *Which one?*, 3) *How many?*, 4) *How much?*

○ 1) Adj (What kind)

◊ <u>Eriberto</u> **/ wears** a *blue* shirt.
    ↑   ↑   ↑
                          PN
    SN   AV   Adj, (What kind of shirt?) = *blue*, modifying PN = *shirt*

○ 2) Adj (Which one)

                          ◊ <u>Aiza</u> **/ owns** *that* car.
    ↑   ↑   ↑
                PN
   SN AV Adj (Which car?) = *that*, modifying PN = *car*

○ 3) Adj (How many)

    ◊ <u>They</u> **/ bought** *five* houses.
      ↑   ↑   ↑   PN
   SPron AV   Adj, (How many?) = *five*, modifying PN = *houses*

○ 4) Adj (How much)

                    ◊ The <u>athletes</u> **/ need** *more* practice.
    ↑   ↑   ↑ PN
 SN   AV   Adj, (How much?) = *more*, modifying PN = *practice*

○ Several adjectives may modify the same noun.

◊ <u>Villa Rosal</u> \ **is** one of *the four seaside* resorts that he owns.
    ↑   ↑   ↑ ↑   ↑ PN

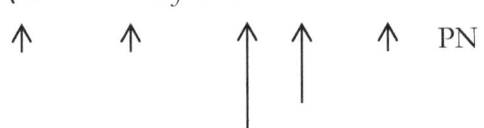

SN   LV   (What kind?) = *seaside,*
                             (How many?) = *four,*
                             determiner or article) = *the*
[Adjective = *the four seaside,* modifying PN = *resorts*]

◊ The *long, golden* <u>rocket</u> /**blasted** off into the *star-studded, outer* space.

SN, singular ↑   AV   ↑(Adj = *long, golden,* modifying SN = <u>rocket</u> ;   Adj = *star- studded, outer.* modifying PN = *space*)

○ The adjectives may modify the subjective noun = tinsmith or the objective noun = car (PN) as in the example above. Adjectives may appear before or after the nouns they modify.

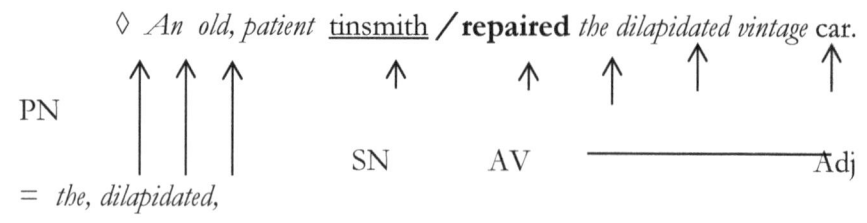

◊ *An old, patient* <u>tinsmith</u> / **repaired** *the dilapidated vintage* car.

PN   ↑ ↑ ↑   ↑   ↑ ↑ ↑   ↑
= *the, dilapidated,*
                  SN   AV   Adj

vintage, modifying PN =

Adj = *an, old, patient,* modifying SN = <u>tinsmith</u>   car

○ The adjectives may modify the subjective noun (tinsmith) or the objective noun (car), as in the example above. Adjectives may *appear before* or *after* the *nouns* they modify. The adjective appearing after the noun is called predicate adjective (PA).

◊   *Hungry* and *exhausted,* the <u>dog</u> / **slumped** to the ground unconsciously.

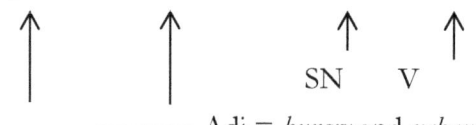

↑   ↑   ↑   ↑
                         SN   V

——————————— Adj = *hungry* and *exhausted,* modifying SN
= <u>dog</u>

◊ <u>Michelle</u>\ **is** *young* and *beautiful.*

SN   LV   Adj (PA) = *young* and *beautiful,*
modifying SN ↑ Michelle ↑   ↑

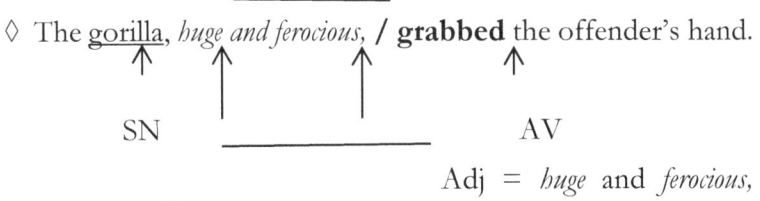

◊ The gorilla, *huge and ferocious,* / **grabbed** the offender's hand.
    ↑   ↑   ↑   ↑

    SN | | AV

                        Adj = *huge* and *ferocious,* modifying SN = gorilla

o An *adjective* does *not appear before* the *pronoun* used as subject of the sentence, except when it is a participial phrase or a compound adjective.

◊ We \ **were** *doubtful* on what he proposed to the council.
  ↑   ↑   ↑

  SPron   LV   predicate Adj (PA) = *doubtful,* modifying SPron = We

◊ *Expressing our doubt on his proposal,* we / **disappointed** him.
      ↑   ↑   ↑

    participial phrase   SPron   AV

      = Adj, *expressing our doubt on his proposal,* modifying SPron = we

   ◊ *Tired and wet,* he **collapsed** on the floor.
  ↑   ↑   ↑

              SPron   AV

Compound Adj = *tired and wet,* modifying SPron = he

□ Exercise 26 : Write the adjectives and the words the adjectives modify as found in the selection.

Safety is an important issue in any discussion of nuclear power. Accidents, like the one at Three Mile Island, are of great concern to the nuclear power industry. But interestingly, that accident along with other smaller problems that have come up in recent years has had an overall positive outcome. The nuclear power industry has learned a great deal from past mistakes. Further, new technology has made a recurrence of the TMI accident extremely remote. The small risk is more than offset by the enormous advantages of nuclear power to the nation's economy.

- **The Articles as Adjectives**

○ The articles *a, an* and *the* are otherwise called *determiners* and function as *adjectives*. *A* and *an* are indefinite articles referring to any one of a class of nouns, while *the* is a definite article referring to a specific noun.

◊ 1) *A* <u>peso</u> \ **is** a big amount to a pauper.

↑ ↑
| SN

Adj, indefinite article = *a, adjective,* modifying <u>peso</u> (*Which peso?* = Any *peso.*)

◊ 2) *An* <u>elephant</u> / **has** a good memory, being a peanut-eating animal.

↑ ↑
| SN

Adj, indefinite article = *an*, modifying N

◊ 3) *The* <u>day</u> \ **seemed** like a year to him.

↑ ↑
| SN

Adj, definite article = *the*, modifying N = <u>day</u> (*Which* day? = The specific or

particular *day.*)

- **Proper Adjectives – Proper Nouns Used as Adjectives**

○ Proper adjectives come from different proper nouns that modify other nouns or used with other nouns. *Proper adjectives* always begin with capital letters.

◊ <u>Eliseo</u> / **drives** a *Tamaraw* truck.

Adj ↑ ↑noun (PN), being modified by *proper*

proper Adj = *Tamaraw* (brand or trade mark), modifying PN =

truck

◊ That \ **is** an *Ilongo* example of entrepreneurship.
↑ ↑

= *Ilongo*

PN, being modified by proper Adj

proper Adj referring to the *native of Iloilo*

□ Common Nouns Used as Adjectives

o Nouns function as adjectives without changing forms. Some grammarians like to call the noun phrase (consisting of two or more nouns) as *double nouns* or *triple nouns*, (as the case may be), that constitute the predicate noun (PN).

◊ Raizza / **likes** to watch *basketball* games.
↑ PN

N, used as Adj, (What kind of games? = *basketball*

games), modifying PN = games

◊ Alejandro / **sent** his friend an *invitation* letter.
↑ PN

N, used as Adj, (What kind of letter? = *invitation* letter), modifying PN = letter

• Possessive Nouns as Adjectives

o Possessive proper nouns that answer the question *Whose?* or *Which?* are adjectives.

◊ *Reynaldo's* bicycle \ **is** very new.
N ↑SN

possessive proper N, Adj (*Whose* bicycle? = *Reynaldo's*), modifying SN = <u>bicycle</u>

o Possessive nouns, *Orlando's* and *coach's,* as adjectives answering the question *Whose?*

◊ *Orlando's* winning playing <u>style</u> / **earned** his *coach's* praise.

    ↑   ↑SN   PN

  possessive proper N = Orlando,   possessive common N = coach,

    Adj,   modifying   SN=   <u>style</u> modifying PN = praise

• Possessive Pronouns Used as Adjectives

o Possessive pronouns show ownership or belonging. They modify nouns or other pronouns

and are called pronominal adjectives.

◊ <u>Digna</u> / **shared** *her* cake with *her* cousins.

    AV   ↑   PN

    pronominal Adj = *her*, modifying PN = *cake* ; second pronoun = *her,*

    modifying cousin (To *whom* the *cake* and *cousins* belong?) ; Prep

    phrase = with her cousins, Adv, modifying AV = **shared**

◊ *Their* <u>team</u> \ **was** the best in *their* league.

  ↑   SN

  pronominal Adj = *their,* modifying SN = team and *their,* modifying league and

    answering question *Whose?*

• Other Pronouns Used as Adjectives

o Indefinite, demonstrative and interrogative pronouns may also function as adjectives. .

Indefinite	Demonstrative	Interrogative
Some	this	which
Many	these	what
Several	that	whose
Few	those	

◊ *Whose* sons **are** *those* boys?

    Adj ↑   ↑ N   ↑ Adj (*Whose* = interrogative pronoun; *those* = demonstrative)

◊ *Many* girls **/ joined** the *few* sessions held.

    ↑   ↑   ↑   N

    Adj N   Adj (*Many* and *few* = indefinite pronouns)

☐ Adverbs – Adverbs modify verbs, adjectives and other adverbs.

• Adverbs are words that modify *verbs, adjectives* or other *adverbs*. Adverbs usually answer the questions *when? how? where? why? how much?* or *how little?* or *to what extent?*

○ *Adverb* modifying *verb*

    ◊ Adv of time (*when?*) = *recently*, modifying the verb = **arrived**) =

He **/ arrived** from Europe *recently*.

◊ Adv of manner (*how?*) = *carefully*, modifying the verb = **drives**) =

Vince **/ drives** *carefully*.

◊ Adv of place (*where?*) = *here*, modifying the verb = **is working** =

Merryl **is working** *here*.

◊ Adv of cause (*why?*) = *because we want to form an association*, modifying the verb =

held = We **/ held** a meeting, *because we want to form an association*.

(Adv = *because we want to form an association*, a dependent clause, modifies the independent clause = We held a meeting.)

◊ Adv of degree (*to what extent?*) = *extremely*, complementing the linking verb = **was**:

The <u>weather</u> \ **was** *extremely* cold.

◊ <u>Rodelo</u> / **speaks** English *fluently*.
　　　　　　　　↑　　　　　　↑
　　　action verb (AV)　　adverb (Adv), modifying AV = **speaks**

◊ The lady / **sang** *melodiously*.
　　　　　　　↑　　↑
　　　AV　　Adv, modifying AV = **sang**

o *Adverb* modifying *adjective*:

◊ They \ **are** *very* fluent English speakers.
　　　　　　↑　　↑
　　　　　Adv　Adj

◊ The song \ **was** *very* melodious.
　　　　　↑　　↑　　↑　　↑
　　SN, singular　LV　Adv　Adj (Adv = *very*, modifying Adj = melodious)

o *Adverb* modifying another *adverb* (*quite*, also called *intensifier*, modifying Adv = *fluently*)

◊ Eda Mae / **speaks** English *quite* fluently.
　　　　　　　　　　　　　　↑　　↑
　　　　　Adv = *quite*, modifying another Adv = *fluently*

◊ The lady / **sang** *quite* melodiously.
　　　↑　　　　　　↑　　↑
　SN, singular　　AV　　Adv, *quite* (*intensifier*), modifying Adv = *melodiously*

◦ *Adverbs* answer the *five questions* about the words or phrases they modify.

◊ **We / read** the instructions *carefully*.

[Adv modifies AV = **read**]
AV   Adv (*In what manner* or *how?* = *carefully*)

◊ They **/ came** *late*.

           AV   Adv (*When* did they *come?* = *late*)

◊ Mario **/ sings** *here*.

      AV   Adv (*Where* does Mario *sing?* = *here*)

◊ The bus **/ arrives** *rarely* at night.

      AV   Adv (*How often* does the *bus arrive?* = *rarely*)

◊ The coffee \ **was** *extremely* hot.

                         PA

     Adv (*To what extent* was the coffee *hot?* = *extremely*)

◦ *Adverbs* modify the entire **verb phrase.**

◊ The whole <u>derelict</u> **/ was being brought** *slowly* to the sea museum.

    AV phrase = **was being brought**   Adv = *slowly*, modifying AV phrase = **was being brought**

◊ The <u>building</u> **/ had been constructed** *defectively*.

           AV phrase   Adv, modifying AV phrase = **had been constructed** (*How was* the building *constructed?* = *defectively*) o *Adverbs* appear at different places in the sentences, (usually at the beginning or end).

◊ *Recently*, a <u>storm</u> / **crossed** the country.

   ↑   ↑
Adv   AV, being modified by Adv *recently*

◊ The lending <u>scheme</u> / **has produced** misunderstanding *frequently*.

                                              ↑

Adv = *frequently*, modifying AV phrase = **has produced**

◊ The <u>boy</u> \ **was** *eagerly* watchful of the comet.

                ↑   ↑
                       Adj

Adv = *eagerly*, modifying Adj = *watchful*

◊ <u>He</u> / **spoke** *quite* haltingly.

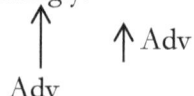

            ↑   ↑Adv
         Adv

[Adv = *quite*, modifying another Adv = *haltingly*]

◊ The <u>man</u> \ **became** *too* fanatically involved in the pseudo-religious group activities.

                       ↑   ↑

Adv = *fanatically*, being modified by *too*

Adv = *too*, (an *intensifier*) modifying another Adv = *fanatically*

• Prepositional Phrases as *Adjectives* or *Adverbs*

o A preposition used together with other parts of speech introducing the phrase function as *adjective* or *adverb* called *adjectival phrase* or *adverbial phrase*, respectively.

o *Prepositional phrase* as *adjective*

    ◊ The <u>girl</u> *with long hair* \ **is** this year's class valedictorian.

SN, singular ↑ ↑

Prep phrase, Adj (Which girl? = *with long hair*, modifying SN = girl)

◊ Rodelyn / **works** as manager *of Riverside Café*.
↑ ↑

PN   Prep phrase, Adj = *of Riverside Café*, modifying

PN = manager

○ *Prepositional phrase* as *adverb*

◊ The scientist / **traveled** *by foot* alone.   [Sentence Pattern = S + V]
↑ ↑

AV   Adv = *by foot*, modifying AV = **traveled**

◊ The hunting group / **departed** late in the afternoon.
↑ ↑

Adv: *late* modifying AV = **departed**   Adv = *in the afternoon*, modifying Adv = *late*)

□ Prepositions. – Prepositions (Prep) are words that express relationship between nouns or pronouns and other words in sentences.

◊ Three books \ **are** *on* the table.
↑

Prep = *on*, telling the relationship of books and table, or telling where the books are in relation to the table (*on* the table)

○ Prepositions are words placed before some noun or pronoun showing relationship. The noun or pronoun following the preposition is called the *object of the preposition*.

◊ The deep sea divers / **find** pearls *beneath* the sea.
↑
Prep phrase = beneath the sea ; object of *Prep*

= *sea*

○ List of some prepositions (Prepositions consisting of more than one word are called *compound prepositions*):

Above behind down near since according to about   below   during of through as of across beneath   except off till as well as against beside for into to in accord with along besides from   onto toward   in front of out of around between in out under in place of prior to at by inside outside over as regards to like before within with despite with regard to in spite of by means of

◊ The <u>theater</u> \ **stands** *in front of* the cultural center.
                         ↑   ↑

compound *Prep* = in front of object of *Prep* = center

◊ The <u>book</u> \ **is** *in* the shelf.
          ↑   ↑ ↑

SN, singular   LV   Prep phrase, completer = *in the shelf*

□ Conjunctions

○ Conjunctions (Conj) are words that connect individual words or group of words

◊ <u>Science</u> *and* <u>technology</u> / **proved** to be both a boon *and* bane to man.
               ↑   ↑

Conj = *and*, connecting noun = *science* noun = to another noun = *technology*

Conj = *and*, connecting boon, to another noun = bane

○ Conjunctions connect group of words (clauses)

◊ <u>We</u> / **must reforest** denuded mountains *or* <u>we</u> / **will make** a desert of our earth.
                                                             ↑

Conj = *or*, connecting two clauses

○ There are three main kinds of conjunctions: *coordinating, correlative* and *subordinating conjunctions*.

○ *Coordinating* conjunctions connect similar parts of speech or words performing the same functions. Coordinating conjunctions are *and, but, for, nor, or, so,* and *yet.*

◊ She \ **is** beautiful, rich *and* intelligent.
　　　　　↑

coordinating Conj = *and*: joining the adjectives = *beautiful, rich* and *intelligent,* being words of equal rank

◊ Brian *and* Val **/ study** Mathematics, Science *and* English every night.
　　　　　　　↑

Conj = *and,* connecting proper nouns

◊ Much **/ was expected** of him, *so* Franco **/ did** his best.
　　　　　　　　　　　　　　　　　↑

Conj = *so,* connecting two independent clauses

◊ Karen **/ went** to the airport to get an incoming package *and* to welcome her cousin.　　　　　　　　　　　　　　　　↑

　Conj = *and,* connecting two verbal phrases

○ *Correlative* conjunctions consist of two or more words that work together as a set. Like coordinating conjunctions, the correlative conjunctions connect words that perform equal functions in a sentence.

either … or …　whether … or …neither … nor …　　not only … but (also) …　　both … and …

◊ The team **/ had** *both* mettle *and* inspiration.
　　　　　　　↑　　　　　↑

correlative Conj = *both, and,* connecting mettle to inspiration

◊ *Either* the captain *or* the sergeants **/ arrived** later.
　　　　　　↑　　　　　　　↑

correlative Conj = *either, or,* connecting two SN captain to sergeant

◊ They **/ will fight,** *or* they **/ will lose.**
　　　　　　　　　　↑

coordinating Conj = *or*, joining two clauses

◊ Phoebe \ is a beautiful *but* chubby girl.
            ↑

coordinating Conj = *but*, joining two Adj = *beautiful* and *chubby*

o *Subordinating* conjunctions connect words to show unequal but important relationships between certain ideas by making one of the ideas subordinate or dependent on the other, i.e., a subordinating Conj connects a dependent clause to an independent (main) clause.

(1) The villagers / **organized** a cooperative, *because* they wanted progress.
                                                        ↑

subordinating Conj = *because*, connecting *they wanted progress* (subordinate) to *The villagers organized a cooperative* (main clause)

o Subordinating conjunctions express relationship of time, manner, cause, condition, comparison, or purpose.

Time Manner Cause Condition Comparison Purpose

After as because although as in order that as as if as long as than so that as long as although even if that as soon as even though before if since provided that until, till through when where unless whenever wherever while while whereas now that in as much as

□ Differentiating Conjunctions from Prepositions

oSometimes identifying subordinating conjunctions is difficult since several of these conjunctions can also function as prepositions or adverbs. Prepositions are always followed by *objects*, conjunctions are not; semi-colons precede conjunctive adverbs coordinating independent clauses and are followed by commas.

◊ The students / **have been practicing** *since* Thursday.
                                              ↑   ↑
Prep = *since*   object of Prep = *Thursday*

◊ Susanita / **likes** to dance; *however*, her mother objects to it vehemently.
                                    ↑

conjunctive Adv = *however*

◊ Consult the members *or* the board of directors *before* you make an official status report.

Conj = *or, before*

☐ Conjunctions and the Structural Sentence Constructions

• Structurally, the sentences are of 1) *simple,* 2) *complex,* 3) *compound,* 4) *compound – complex and* 5) *compound – compound constructions.*

1) Simple sentence – made up of one independent clause having one subject and one predicate

◊ <u>Tourists</u> **/ flock** to Iloilo City in January to watch the Dinagyang Festival.

    SN   AV

◊ <u>She</u> **/ likes** to ride on the motorized water ski.

  SPron   AV

2) Complex sentence – made up of one independent clause and one dependent clause

◊ The <u>rebels</u> **/ signed** a peace agreement, *because* <u>they</u> **/ wanted** peace.

           SN   AV (Independent clause = The rebels signed a peace agreement dependent clause = *because* they wanted peace)

◊ As the shipwrecked <u>victims</u> **/ were losing** hope of surviving, the <u>rescuers</u> **/ came** to save them from death in the icy waters.

SN AV

(Independent clause = The rescuers came to save them from death in the icy waters; dependent clause = as the shipwrecked victims were losing hope of surviving)

3) Compound sentence – consists of two independent clauses

◊ Two <u>brothers</u> **/ joined** the soft drink drinking contest *and* the elder <u>boy</u> / **won** first prize.

(Independent clauses connected by conjunction = *and*)

4) Compound–complex sentence – consists of two independent clauses and one dependent clause

◊ The <u>husband</u> / **cooked** the meat *and* his <u>wife</u> / **prepared** sandwich, while their teenage

<u>son</u> / **leaned** on a tree trunk to sleep.

(Two independent clauses = The <u>husband</u> / **cooked** the meat *and* his <u>wife</u> /

prepared sandwich ; dependent clause = while their teenage <u>son</u> / **leaned** on a

tree trunk to sleep)

5) Compound–compound sentence – consists of four clauses connected by correlative

conjunctions (Compound – compound sentence constructions are very rare.)

◊ The <u>candidates</u> / **came** to the village in a helicopter *and* the <u>people</u> / **ran** to meet them;

the <u>teeners</u> / **were** greatly **disappointed** – their <u>actor-idol</u> / **did** not **come.**

◊ <u>Lightning</u> / **flashed** like fiery ribbons in the sky; <u>thunders</u> / **roar** in deafening

crescendo; <u>Jessie</u> / **pressed** hard the remote ignition switch, *and* the yellow <u>rocket</u> /

cut a swath of smoke vertically into the sky and **plummeted** into the frothing sea in

a flash. (and plummeted into the frothing sea in a flash = dependent clause)

☐ Verbals and Verbal Phrases

• Verbals are forms of verbs that function as 1) *adjectives*, 2) *adverbs* and 3) *nouns*, but no longer as verbs. However, verbals retain some of the properties of verbs, express actions or take direct objects, indirect objects, predicate nominatives or predicate adjectives. A verbal cannot be a predicate verb; it can't make a statement or ask a question.

• Three classes of verbals: 1) *Infinitive*, or the **to form**, 2) *Participles*, or the **–ed, –en** and **–ing forms**, and 3) *Gerund*, or the **–ing form** of the verb – The *infinitive* or the **to + base** form (or the *to form*) functions as *adjective, adverb* or *noun*. The *–ed, –en* forms (past participles) and *–ing* form (present participle) are used as *adjectives* to *modify nouns* and as *adverbs* to *modify verbs*. The *gerund* is used as noun subject or object.

☐ Infinitive Verbal Phrases

• The infinitive is a verbal that has three elements. The verb is (1) usually preceded by the preposition *to*, as in *to sing* (2) in the base form (*sing*), and (3) in the present tense, as in *smile* or in the perfect tense, *to have loved*. The infinitive is used as a noun, an adjective or an adverb. (The base form of the verb even without the preposition *to* is an infinitive.)

• 1) The *infinitive* as a verbal is the result of putting the preposition *to* before the *base form* of the verb. = *to complain* (*to* = preposition ; *complain* = verb base form)

◊ Reno **/ is going** *to write* his brother a letter.
　　　　　　　　　　↑

infinitive = *to write (base form* of the verb = *write*, preceded by the preposition *to), as noun object* of AV phrase = **is going**

• The base form of the verb is an *infinitive* without the preposition *to*.

◊ The teacher **/ helps** *discuss* the topic on development in the barangay meeting.
　　　　　　　　　↑

infinitive = *discuss (*in place of *to discuss)*

• The *infinitive* as 1) *noun*, 2) *adjective*, and 3) *adverb*

○ 1) The *infinitive*, as subject noun

　　◊ To complain \ **is** useless.
　　◊ A complaint \ **is** useless.
　　SN, singular　　LV
　　SN, singular　　LV

○ 1a) The *infinitive*, as predicate noun (PN)

◊ <u>To die</u> \ **is** *to rest*.

    SN   LV   PN   (PN = *to rest*)

◊ <u>To love</u> \ **is** a many-splendored *thing*.   ◊ <u>Love</u> \ **is** a many-splendored *thing*.

    SN   LV   PN   SN   LV

○ 1b) The *infinitive*, as <u>object of preposition</u>

    ◊ <u>She</u> / **did** nothing except <u>sing</u>. (*to sing*)

    SPron   AV   Prep   Obj of preposition   (Prep = except)

○ 1c) The *infinitive*, as <u>direct object</u>

    ◊ The <u>platoon</u> / **was ordered** *to reconnoiter* the area.

    SN   AV phrase   DO   (DO = *to reconnoiter*)

○ 1d) The *infinitive*, as <u>appositive</u>

◊ <u>Ceres' motion</u> *<u>to cancel</u>* the schedule / **was not approved**.

    SN   Appositive= *to cancel*   AV

○ 1e) The *infinitive*, as *delayed subject* (Sentence begins with "it," an expletive)

    ◊ <u>It</u> \ **seems** logical *to entertain* a wild guess. (<u>To entertain</u> a wild guess \ **seems** logical.)

SPron   LV   Infinitive   SN   LV

○ 2a) The *infinitive*, as <u>adjective</u>, modifying the *subject*

◊ His <u>attempt</u> *to sing* alone / **was not allowed** by his peers.
          ↑   ↑

    SN, singular   infinitive = *to sing*, as Adj, modifying SN = attempt

○ The *infinitive*, as <u>adjective</u>, modifying the *object*

◊ <u>Sonia</u> / **did not consider** her chance *to win* in the contest.

    SN   AV   DO   Adj, *to win* = infinitive used as adjective modifying the object *chance*

o 3) The *infinitive,* as adverb = *to fight,* modifying an *action verb* and 3a) an *adjective*

◊ Rolly **/ volunteered** *to fight.*

SN, singular   AV   infinitive = *to fight,* as Adv, modifying AV = **volunteered**

◊ "Only those who are not afraid *to die* \ **are** fit *to live.*

SPron, plural   infinitive as Adv = *to die,*   (completer = fit to live), *to live* is

modifying Adj = *afraid*   also Adv, modifying Adj = *fit*

□ Participles

• Participles, like the infinitives, are verb forms that function also as noun, adjective and adverb. There are two kinds of participles, which are the past participle and the present participle. The *past participle* is the past form or the *–ed* form (or *–en* form) of the verb. The *present participle* is the present progressive form of the verb (ending in *–ing*) or the *–ing* verb.

o *The Past Participle as Noun (N)* - The *past participle* (–ed form of the regular verb), like adjective *poor* or *rich*, is also used as *noun*. As SN, the *participle* is primarily used in the *plural sense*. The –en form (irregular verb) is used in similar manner.

◊ The wounded **/ were attended** to by the medics. (*wounded* men)

SN, plural   AV phrase

◊ The retarded **/ were separated** from the fast learners. (*retarded* children)

SN, plural   AV phrase

◊ The unseen **/ inhabit** the old mansion.   (*unseen* spirits)

SN, plural   AV

o *The Present Participle as Adjective (Adj)*

◊ The *visiting* <u>diplomat</u> / **donated** books to the school.

   Adj,   SN   AV

      present participle = *visiting*, modifying SN = <u>diplomat</u>

◊ *Looking pale and weak*, <u>Fredelina</u> / **admitted** to her being drunk.

   Adj phrase,   SN   AV

      participial phrase = *looking pale and weak,* modifies SN = <u>Fredelina</u>

(In the example above, *visiting* is a present participle; although functioning as adjective it retains the properties of verbs and expresses action [present progressive tense form of the verb *visit*]. The second present participle, *looking* is part of the participial phrase as Adj, modifying SN = Fredelina.)

o The *Past Participle as Adverb (Adv)*

◊ <u>Timothy</u> / **stopped** *dead* in his tracks in view of the big snake.

   SN   AV   Adv, past participle = *dead,* modifying the verb = **stopped**

◊ <u>Dario</u> / **cooked** *fried* all the fish.

   SN   AV   Adv, past participle = *fried,* modifying the verb = **cooked**

◊ <u>Diego</u> / **operated** *overdriven* his new stereo.

   SN   AV   Adv, past participle = *overdriven,* modifying the verb = **operated**

o *The Present Participle as Adverb (Adv)*

◊ The <u>tiger</u> / **charged** *growling* through the crowd.

   SN   AV   Adv, present participle = *growling,* modifies the verb **charged**

◊ The hungry <u>baby</u> / **continued** *crying* in the nursery room.

          SN   AV   Adv, present participle = *crying*, modifying the verb **continued**

☐ Avoiding Dangling Participial Phrase Modifiers

• When the participle is a phrase, care must be observed to avoid hanging or dangling ludicrously the phrase modifier. The participial phrase, used as adjective introducing the sentence, must modify the subject as shown in the following examples.

(1) *Dangling: Rounding the narrow alley corner*, the condominium \ **appeared** *colossal.*

participial phrase, SN   LV   PA

Adj = *rounding the narrow alley corner*

(Who went around the alley corner? If it is the subject (*condominium*) that went around the alley corner, then the modifier is *not dangling.*)

(2) *Right: Rounding the narrow alley corner,* we / **saw** the colossal condominium.

          ↑   ↑   ↑

    participial phrase,j   SPron   AV   DO

Adj = *rounding the narrow alley corner,* modifying SPron = we

(3) *Dangling: Stone dead and headless,* the crocodile / **ate** the monkey.

        participial phrase, Adj =   SN   AV   DO

       stone dead and headless, modifying SN = crocodile

(Can you imagine the *stone dead and headless* crocodile **eating** the monkey?)

(4) *Right: Stone dead and headless,* the monkey / **was eaten** by the crocodile.

        participial phrase, Adj =   SN   AV phrase

    stone dead and headless, modifying SN = monkey

• The verbal as *modifier* (phrase) must be placed *close* to the doer of the action *to avoid* a *ridiculous situation,* as suggested by the sentence.

○ *Dangling* = The singer, on the shiny new convertible car, *smiling broadly,* / **waved** to her fans.
AV

SN, singular   Adj,↑ (participial phrase ↑=
smiling broadly, modifying
Adj, prep phraise = on the SN |= singer; Adv = broadly shiny new convertible car, modifying adj = *smiling* modifying SN = singer

(Probe questions: *Which is smiling? Is it the car* or the *singer?*)

○ Clear = *Smiling* broadly on the shiny new convertible car, the singer, / **waved** to her fans.

↑   ↑

Adj = (action SN, singular AV verb, regular, -- ing verb present participle = participial phrase = *smiling* broadly), modifying SN = singer)

☐ Participial Phrase Used in Closing a Letter Is Incorrect

• A participial phrase used in closing a letter is incorrect, because it is a dangling modifier.

(1)   *Dangling* = *Hoping* for your usual consideration.

Very truly yours,

(signature over printed name 2 double spaces after)

(2) *Right*: *Hoping* for your usual consideration, I \ **am**/
subject pronoun = I   Very truly yours,   ↑ ↑
                             linking verb = **am**

(The main clause is = I \ **am** *very truly yours, Ernesto L. Lasafin.*)

(Note: The correct sentence consists of the participial phrase = *Hoping for your kind consideration,* (present participle) and the main clause = *I am very truly yours.* The end-part of the complete sentence is the signatory close *Very truly yours,* followed by the *name of the letter writer* 2 spaces after. However, Example (2) is passé, hence, its use is being discouraged. Using a modifying word for *appreciated* is also in bad taste, *appreciaton,* like *consideration* is not made in degrees, it's always whole and indivisible.)

(3) *Better*: Your usual consideration is appreciated.

Very truly yours,

(Signature, two double spaces after)

☐ Gerunds

• *Gerunds* are the *–ing* forms of the verbs used as *nouns*.

◊ <u>Teaching</u> \ **is** a noble *profession*.

SN LV PN

◊ <u>Watching television</u> / **takes** most of his time. (*Watching* is a noun inseparable from SN AV *television* as the subject noun, hence it is part of the gerund phrase.)

• The *gerund*, being a verb form, can be modified by an *adverb*, as in <u>dancing</u> *merrily*.

◊ <u>Dancing</u> *merrily* \ **is** her pastime. (*Merrily* is an adverb that modifies the gerund SN Adv LV <u>dancing</u>. Dancing is a noun, but being an –ing verb it retains the property of the verb that allows its being modified by an adverb.)

◊ <u>Singing</u> *loudly* \ **is** his way of letting out his pent up emotion.

    ↑   ↑   ↑

SN, singular, | LV

gerund   Adv = *loudly*, modifying the gerund = <u>singing</u>,
an **–ing** verb

☐ Exercise 23 : List down the *verbals* and *identify*.

1. Flying alone, he / reached Papua.

2. Any regulated drug / cannot be sold without a doctor's prescription.

3. His torn kite / dived to the ground.

4. A horse / lies crippled on the street.

5. The whale / remains frozen in the lake.

6. The scheming lady / came clapping and laughing deliriously to the stage.

7. My coffee \ is piping hot.

8. Monita / arrived hiking.

9. Singing \ is Mark's favorite hobby.

10. Precy/ dislikes eating sea shells.

☐ Split Infinitive – an infinitive verb form with an *element*, usually an adverb, *interposed* between *to* and the *verb,* producing a clumsy effect.

o *Split Infinitive* = <u>Rona</u> **/ decided** *<u>to</u>* unconditionally *<u>accept</u>* the terms.
↑   ↑ ↑   ↑   ↑

        SN, singular   AV   Prep   Adv   verb (base form)

o *Better* = <u>Rona</u> **/ decided** *<u>to</u> <u>accept</u>* the terms unconditionally.
↑   ↑   ↑   ↑

  SN, singular   AV   infinitive   Adv

o Wrong = <u>We</u> **/ have** a plan *<u>to</u> gradually, systematically* and *economically <u>relieve</u>* the burden.
                                   ↑   ↑   ↑

  Adv, (separating the infinitive = *to relieve*)

o *Right* = <u>We</u> **/ have** a plan *<u>to relieve</u>* the burden *gradually, systematically* and *economically.*
                             ↑   ↑   ↑

       infinitive *(to relieve)*   Adv

• Care must be exercised to avoid *<u>split infinitive</u>*, lest the meaning intended is distorted or ambiguity is created -- the adverb must modify what is intended to be modified to preclude awkward passages.

o *Split Infinitive*:

Correct:

◊ 1) *<u>to</u>* really *<u>be</u>* sure

◊ *<u>to</u> <u>be</u>* really sure

◊ 2) *<u>to</u>* just *<u>have</u>* seen

◊ *<u>to</u> <u>have</u>* just seen

- *Acceptable to a few.*
- ◊ 3) If you want *to* really *help* the patient, you must understand his feelings.
- *Not* accept*a*ble:
- ◊ *To* better *understand* the miners' plight, he worked with them in the mines.
- *Acceptable*:
- ◊ We expect our output *to* more than *double* in a year.

□ Mood of the Verb or Speaker's Attitude toward Factuality or Likelihood of Action

- 1. Indicative mood – states a fact or asks a question
- ◊ (1) Don Fernando **is** a philanthropist.
- ◊ (2) If there is time, we **can visit** Sicogon.
- ◊ (3) **Does** Cynthia **collect** coins?
- 2. Imperative mood – expresses a command, desire or an urgent request
- ◊ (1) Please **tell** us a story, Lolo. (request)   ◊ (2) **March**!   (command)
- 3. Subjunctive mood – states a condition contrary to fact or wish; indicated by *if, as if, as though*. In parliamentary expression, the verb in the *dependent clause* is in the *past time;* in *demand,* the verb in the *dependent clause,* (introduced by that), is in the present time.

◊ *Wish* :   *If* I **were** *to become President*, you would be my Executive Secretary.

◊ *Contrary to fact* :   Rey would join the excursion *if he* **had** *a motorcycle*.

◊ *Parliamentary expression* :   I move *that he* **be named** *the manager*.

◊ *Demand* :   The rule requires *that he* **present** the needed qualification.

□ Exercise 24 : Make the *verb* agree with its *subject*.

1. The boys / [joins / join] the cadet drill every day.

2. They / [fights / fight] bravely for their country.

3. Dina / [works / work] as a nurse in her village.

4. Mike / [drives / drive] like hell in winning car races.

5. The message / [convey / conveys] a very strong warning to the rebels.

6. The dog / [watches / watch] over its master's grave.

7. Sev / dash / dashes to catch up with Celso.

8. Dindo / [catches / catch] frogs for sale to food gourmands.

9. Milo / [teaches / teach] vocational and technical courses for the blind.

10. The president / [veto / vetoes] the bill enacted by congress in a republican government.

11. Ram / [cooes / coo] like a dove to win Marsha's heart.

12. Fe / [flies / fly] home every Saturday from Hong Kong.

13. The baby / [cries / cry] a lot every morning.

14. Brix / [choose / chooses] Riga over Garda.

☐ Exercise 25 : Identify the verb phrases in bold type as to *time* and *voice*

1. I / **am depressed** by the sad events in the family.

2. Some books / **were stolen** from the library.

3. I / **am reading** my textbook

4. The students / **are studying** their lessons for final test.

5. Mar / **is building** a treehouse.

6. The girls / **were dancing** when we passed by the auditorium.

7. Bob / **was washing** the car.

8. The boys / **have informed** their parents about their educational trip.

9. Vicente **/ has written** his brother about his new job.

10. They **/ have been teaching** modern math for ten years now.

11. Nimia **/ has been caring** for her sick mother until her sister took over.

☐ More Pointers on Subject and Verb Agreement

○ Prepositional phrase modifiers or *substantives* found in the subject area referred to as *intervening words between* the *subject* and the *verb*, usually set off by commas, do not affect the number of the subject.

◊ 1) The schools superintendent, *along with some supervisors,* **/ arrives** for the sports meet.

>SN, singular = superintendent ; AV, simple present time = **arrives**, agreeing with

singular SN = superintendent

◊ 2) The soldiers, *with their commander,* **/ plan** to attack the rebel stronghold.

>SN, plural = soldiers ; AV, simple present time = **plan**, agreeing with plural SN = soldiers

◊ 3) Jose Rizal, *not Andres Bonifacio,* **/ deserves** the honor as the national hero.

>SN, singular = Jose Rizal ; AV, simple present time = **deserves**, agreeing with

singular SN = Jose Rizal

◊ 4) One *of the girls who are off-key* in singing \ **is** Eloise.

>SN, singular = one ; LV, present time, be = **is**, agreeing with singular SN = one

○ Prepositional phrases between the subject and verb do not affect the number of the subject.

◊ 1) Agreement *of subjects with their verbs and pronouns with their antecedents* \ **is** essential to clear and effective writing.

>SN, singular = agreement; LV, present time, be = **is**, agreeing with singular SN = agreement

◊ 2) *The* arrangement *of the office records* **/ proves** to be a backbreaking work for Cynthia.

>SN, singular = arrangement ; AV, simple present time = **proves**, agreeing with

singular SN = arrangement

◊ 3) *The greatest* part *of his investments* **/ is found** in real estate.

>SN, singular = part ; AV phrase, present time = **is found**, agreeing with singular

SN = part

○ Compound subjects joined by the conjunction *and* require verbs in the plural form; likewise, a subject noun modified by two or more adjectives that give different meanings needs a verb in the plural form.

◊ 1) Antonio *and* I **/ were elected** directors of the cooperative.

>SN, plural = Antonio *and* I ; AV phrase, past time = **were elected**, agreeing with

plural SN = Antonio *and* I

◊ 2) *A* man *and a* boy **/ catch** frogs for a living.

>SN, plural = man *and* boy ; AV, simple present time = **catch**, agreeing with plural

SN = man *and* boy

◊ 3) *Many a* boy *and a* girl **/ have sat** under this mango tree.

>SN, plural = boy *and* girl ; AV phrase, present perfect time = **have sat**, agreeing with plural SN = boy *and* girl

◊ 4) Filipino *and* Arabian music \ **are** entirely different.

>SN, plural = Filipino *and* Arabian music ; LV, present time, *be* = **are**, agreeing with plural SN = Filipino *and* Arabian music

◊ 5) Gunboat diplomacy *and* mailed fist policy \ **are** complementary evils of foreign relations.

>SN, plural = gunboat diplomacy *and* mailed fist policy ; LV, present time, *be* = **are**, agreeing with plural SN = gunboat diplomacy *and* mailed fist policy

Exception 1) The singular subjects connected by *and* or *but*, and set off in contrast with the other, require a verb in singular form as they really belong to separate statements or propositions.

◊ 1) <u>Honesty</u> *and not* <u>influence</u> \ **is** responsible for his success in life.

>SN, singular = <u>honesty</u> ; LV, present time, *be* = **is**, agreeing with <u>singular</u> SN = <u>honesty</u>

◊ 2) *Not* <u>interest</u> *in job but* <u>ambition</u> / **leads** to his promotion.

>SN, singular = <u>interest</u> ; AV, simple present time = **leads**, agreeing with <u>singular</u>

SN = <u>interest</u>

Exception 2) The singular subjects joined by *and* referring to the same person or thing, or together they refer to a single unit (one is the essential and indispensable part of the other) need singular verb.

◊ 1) <u>Coffee</u> *and* <u>cream</u> \ **is** my usual morning fare.

>SN, singular = <u>coffee</u> *and* <u>cream</u> ; LV, present time, *be* = **is**, agreeing with <u>singular</u>

SN = <u>coffee</u> *and* <u>cream</u>

◊ 2) <u>Green</u> *and* <u>gold</u>, *as colors* / **was adopted** by the class as their class banner.

>SN, singular = <u>green</u> and <u>gold</u> ; AV phrase, past time = **was adopted**, agreeing with <u>singular</u> SN = <u>green</u> and <u>gold</u>

◊ 3) <u>Rice</u> *and* <u>fish</u> / **constitutes** the daily breakfast among most of the Filipinos.

>SN, singular = <u>rice</u> *and* <u>fish</u> ; AV, simple present time = **constitutes**, agreeing with <u>singular</u> SN = <u>rice</u> *and* <u>fish</u>

Exception 3) The words in the subjects joined by *and* but preceded by *each* or *every* (aggregating adjective) need verbs singular form.

◊ 1) *Each* <u>man</u> *and* <u>woman</u> / **was required** to register for membership at the club office.

>SN, singular = *each* <u>man</u> *and* <u>woman</u> ; AV phrase, past time = **was required**, agreeing with <u>singular</u> SN = *each* <u>man</u> *and* <u>woman</u>

◊ 2) *Every* <u>report</u> *and* <u>account</u> *of what happened* **/ was being scrutinized** by the task force.

>SN, singular = *every* <u>report</u> *and* <u>account</u> ; AV phrase, past time = **was being scrutinized**, agreeing with <u>singular</u> SN = *every* <u>report</u> *and* <u>account</u>

◊ 3) *Many a* <u>man</u> **/ likes** to spend time with a beautiful woman.

>SN, singular = <u>man</u> ; AV, simple present time = **likes**, agreeing with <u>singular</u> SN = <u>man</u>

Exception 4) The singular words in the compound subjects using *either… or, neither…nor,* or *not… but* need verbs in singular form. When the compound subject combines a singular and plural subjects, the verb agrees with the nearest noun or pronoun.

◊ 1) *Either* <u>Loreto</u> *or* <u>Digna</u> **/ was informed** of their uncle's arrival

>SN, singular = <u>Digna</u> ; AV phrase, past time = **was informed**, agreeing with

<u>singular</u> SN = <u>Digna</u>

◊ 2) *Neither* <u>they</u> *nor* <u>she</u> **/ is doing** the painting project.

>SPron, singular = <u>she</u> ; AV phrase, present time = **is doing**, agreeing with <u>singular</u>

Pron = <u>she</u>

◊ 3) *Not the* <u>intruders</u> *but the* <u>guard</u> **/ has destroyed** the window.

>SN, singular = <u>guard</u> ; AV phrase, present perfect time = **has destroyed**, agreeing with <u>singular</u> SN = <u>guard</u>

◊ 4) *Either the* <u>crewmembers</u> *or the* <u>pilot</u> **/ was notified** of the change in the flight

schedule.

>SN, singular = <u>pilot</u> ; AV phrase, past time = **was notified**, agreeing with <u>singular</u>

SN = <u>pilot</u>

◊ 5) *Neither the* <u>captain</u> *nor the* <u>soldiers</u> \ **are** aware of the enemy camp by the hillside.

>SN, plural = soldiers ; LV, present time, *be* = **are**, agreeing with plural SN = soldiers

○Pronouns *each, every, anybody, anyone, either, neither, everyone, someone, somebody, one, no one, none, nobody, etc.,* need verbs in singular form.

◊ 1) No one **/ was seen** in the area where he was discovered dead.

>SPron, singular = no one ; AV phrase, past time = **was seen**, agreeing with singular

SPron = no one

◊ 2) Neither **/ admits** the crime charged despite the overwhelming evidence.

>SPron, singular = neither ; AV phrase, simple present time = **admits**, agreeing with singular SPron = neither

○Nouns denoting amount or quantity that can be counted or idea of being countable, take plural verbs.

◊ 1) Almost one-third of the violent protest marchers **/ were detained** by the police

>SN, plural = one-third ; AV phrase, past time = **were detained**, agreeing with plural SN one-third

◊ 2) Half of the rice in the warehouse **/ was eaten** by weevils.

>SN, singular = half ; AV phrase, past time = **was eaten**, agreeing with singular SN = half

◊ 3) *A big* amount *of the stolen rice* **/ was lost** when the ship sank.

>SN, singular = amount ; AV phrase, past time = **was lost**, agreeing with singular SN = amount

◊ 4) One-third of the population of Lambunao **/ live** in the mountainous area.

>SN, plural = one-third ; AV phrase, simple present time = **live**, agreeing with plural SN = one-third

○ Nouns using the phrase *a* number *of* need verb in plural form; *the* number, singular form.

◊ 1) <u>A number</u> of malnourished children **/ were fed** milk and nutribun by the foundation.

>SN, plural = <u>a number</u> ; AV phrase, past time = **were fed**, agreeing with <u>plural</u> SN = <u>a number</u>

◊ 2) <u>The number</u> *of boys* **/ exceeds** the number of the girls present in the acquaintance party.

>SN, singular = *the* <u>number</u> ; AV, simple present time = **exceeds**, agreeing with <u>singular</u> SN = *the* <u>number</u>

○ Collective nouns referred to as a *whole* require verbs in the singular form; if considered as individual persons or things collective nouns need verbs in the plural form.

◊ 1) The <u>Air Force</u> **/ has trained** pilots for the airline industry.

>SN, singular = <u>Air Force</u>; AV phrase, present perfect time = **has trained**, agreeing

with <u>singular</u> SN = <u>Air Force</u>

◊ 2) The <u>Army</u> **/ differ** in their opinions about human rights abuses.

>SN, plural = <u>Army</u> ; AV, simple present time = **differ**, agreeing with <u>plural</u> SN = <u>Army</u>

*<u>Pants</u>, <u>trousers</u>, <u>scissors</u>, <u>pliers</u>, <u>shears</u>, <u>tongs</u>, etc., are plural nouns that require verbs in the plural form. The phrase *a <u>pair</u> of* ... (before the noun) makes these plural nouns singular.

◊ 1) <u>Denim pants</u> costing five pesos in the early '50s **/ sell** at a thousand pesos now.

>SN, plural = <u>denim pants</u> ; AV, simple present time = **sell**, agreeing with <u>plural</u> SN = <u>denim pants</u>

◊ 2) <u>Tongs</u> **/ are made** by local blacksmiths who work for a cooperative.

>SN, plural = <u>tongs</u> ; AV, present time = **are made**, agreeing with <u>plural</u> SN = <u>tongs</u>

◊ 3) *The* <u>scissors</u> *used in ribbon-cutting* \ **were** dull, so that the mayor got angry with his aide.

\>SN, plural = <u>scissors</u> ; LV, past time, *be* = **were**, agreeing with <u>plural SN</u> = <u>scissors</u>

o Some nouns *ending in -s* are singular in number and require verbs in singular form.

◊ 1) <u>Statistics</u> \ **is** a subject shunned by students.

>SN, singular = <u>statistics</u> ; LV, present time, *be* = **is**, agreeing with <u>singular</u> SN =

<u>statistics</u>

◊ 2) The <u>whereabouts</u> *of the murderers* **/ baffles** the police.

>SN, singular = <u>whereabouts</u> ; AV, simple present time = **baffles**, agreeing with

<u>singular</u> SN = <u>whereabouts</u>

◊ 3) *The* <u>news</u> *on the calamity* **/ worries** many people.

>SN, singular = <u>news</u> ; AV, simple present time = **worries**, agreeing with <u>singular</u>

SN = <u>news</u>

◊ 4) <u>Aerobics</u> \ **is** a good exercise for the elderly.

>SN, singular = <u>aerobics</u> ; LV, present time, *be* = **is**, agreeing with <u>singular</u> SN = <u>aerobics</u>

o Plural nouns indicating weight, extent or quantity need verbs in singular form.

◊ 1) <u>Ten miles</u> \ **appears** to be a very long distance to an octogenarian.

>SN, singular = <u>ten miles</u> ; LV, present time = **appears**, agreeing with <u>singular</u> SN = <u>ten miles</u>

◊ 2) <u>Fifty pesos</u> \ **is** a big sum to a miser.

>SN, singular = <u>fifty pesos</u> ; LV, present time, *be* = **is**, agreeing with <u>singular</u> SN = <u>fifty pesos</u>

3) <u>Five tons</u> **/ was deducted** from the total tonnage capacity of the bridge.

>SN, singular = <u>five tons</u> ; AV phrase, past time = **was deducted**, agreeing with <u>singular</u> SN = <u>five tons</u>

o In sentence construction where the verb appears ahead of the subject, care must be observed lest one makes the verb agree with the noun in the predicate or complement side.

◊ 1) Under the tree branch **hang** the <u>bats</u>.

>SN, plural = <u>bats</u> ; AV, simple present time = **hang**, agreeing with <u>plural</u> SN = <u>bats</u>

◊ 2) There **go** *the* <u>general</u> *and his* <u>aide</u>.

>SN, plural = <u>general</u> *and* <u>aide</u> ; AV, simple present time = **go**, agreeing with <u>plural</u> SN = <u>general</u> *and* <u>aide</u>

◊ 3) Here **come** <u>Violy</u> *and* <u>Rey</u> to join the alumni homecoming.

>SN, plural = <u>Violy</u> *and* <u>Rey</u> ; AV, simple present time = **come**, agreeing with <u>plural</u> SN = <u>Violy</u> *and* <u>Rey</u>

◊ 4) There **marches** the <u>queen</u>, together with her court.

>SN, singular = queen ; AV, simple present time = **marches**, agreeing with <u>singular</u> SN = <u>queen</u>

*Parallel Structure of Sentences – Parallel structure of phrases or words connected by conjunctions in the compound parts of the sentence must be observed.

Correct: I <u>will</u> not <u>kiss</u> you nor <u>will</u> I <u>give</u> you a gift.

Incorrect: Maita <u>does</u> <u>exercise</u> and to <u>jog</u> every morning.

Correct: Maita does exercise and jogging every morning.

Incorrect: He prefers <u>to</u> <u>fish</u> to <u>hunting</u> games.

Correct: The kid prefers <u>playing</u> to <u>doing</u> chores..

Incorrect: Rina's hobbies are <u>cooking</u>, <u>baking</u> and <u>to</u> <u>paint</u>. (Use painting instead of to paint.)

☐ Use of the Comma

- The use of punctuations is very important in effective communication. Punctuations help make clear the meaning of words or group of words. The use of the punctuation mark called the *period* completes a sentence, but a *comma* can change the meaning of the ideas presented by the sentence.

(1) The pig / **eats** shoots and leaves. (The pig is an animal that feeds on plant shoots and leaves.)

(2) The pig / **eats, shoots,** and **leaves.** (The pig is a derogatory reference to a brazen man, usually, a bad cowboy.)

Thus, it is necessary that we review some salient points in the use of all punctuation marks for clarity in getting our messages across to our readers or listeners.

o1) The comma is used after an adverbial dependent clause that precedes the independent or main clause.   A comma is used to separate the dependent adverbial clause that follows the main clause.

◊ Comma needed: *As soon as the data was received,* they / **were encoded** in the computer.

◊ No comma used: The councilors promptly / **approved** the ordinance *when the sponsors justified its necessity to help combat crime.*

o2) The comma is used after a participial phrase or an absolute phrase that begins a sentence.

◊ Participial phrase: *Running away in fear of the frog,* Jocelyn / **lost** her purse.

◊ Absolute phrase: *Having ended their meeting,* the group / **took** their good night's rest.

o3) The comma is used after an introductory infinitive, but not when the infinitive phrase is the subject.

◊ Infinitive phrase: *To win in an election,* you / **must** spend a lot of money.

◊ Infinitive phrase as subject: *To win in an election* \ **was** his dream.

o4) The comma is used to set off parenthetical phrases, clauses and transitional words like however, moreover, consequently, etc.

◊ Phrase: *Of course*, there are many ways to kill a chicken.

◊ Clause: Anyone, *I believe*, can do the same thing.

◊ Transitional word: *Therefore,* we can have no other conclusion than this one.

◊ Explanatory clause: The President believes he won in an honest election, *and we agree with him,* to remain in office until his term expires.

o5) Introductory expressions are separated with a comma, such as *yes, surely, indeed,* well, etc.

◊ *Yes,* it's Peter who won. *Very well,* we will join you as soon as the rain stops.

o6) Nonrestrictive clause that is not essential to complete the meaning of a sentence is separated by commas.

◊ Perlita, who lives in Jaro, married Leo.

o7) An appositive is separated by a comma from the rest of the sentence.

◊ Magno, a family friend, went to Saudi Arabia.

o8) Words in direct addresses are set off by a comma.

◊ Lydia, please take this gift to Grandmother.

- O -

Some Common Expressions In English Usage

Ace Up One's Sleeve – *Information kept in reserve that will purportedly win one's case or cause* is the meaning of this phrase.

Ex. (1) The police chief has an <u>ace up his sleeves</u> against the suspected drug lord.

<u>Acid Test</u> – The meaning of this phrase is *ultimate test*.

Ex. (1) The neophyte passed the <u>acid test</u> for membership in the fraternity.

<u>Acquit Oneself</u> – This expression means *to show one's quality or good conduct and succeed in getting out of a predicament.*

Ex. (1) Marco <u>acquitted himself</u> as stage artist despite the discouragement he went through.

<u>Address Oneself To</u> – *To apply oneself to a task* is the meaning of this expression.

Ex. (1) Corazon <u>addresses herself to</u> her household chores early in the morning every day.

<u>Advocate</u> – *Advocate*, which means *to support*, needs *no preposition* as a transitive verb.

Ex. (1) Rogelio <u>advocated</u> a socialist form of government.

<u>Agree With</u>; <u>Agree To</u> – Using *agree with* a person and *agree to* an idea makes good sentences.

Ex. (1) He <u>agreed with</u> Sim on the matter.

(2) Sheila <u>agreed to</u> his proposition.

(3) The weather does not <u>agree with</u> me.

<u>Alive and Kicking</u> – *Sprightly and much alert* is the meaning of this phrase.

Ex. (1) Despite his age, Lauro is alive and kicking.

All Ready; Already; All Right, not Alright – The adverb *all right* should not be written as *alright* to mean *okay*; *alright* is not yet accepted as good English. It must not be confused with *already* and *all ready* which are both good adverbs.

Ex. (1) What you did is all right; strike while the iron is hot.

(2) Ren already prepared the menu before you came.

(3) We arrive all ready for the game. They appeared all ready to go?

Allow For; Allow Of – *Allow* with the preposition *for* means *to plan with adequate margin*, while *allow of* is *to permit or admit something to take place*.

Ex. (1) The engineer allowed for a big margin in the cost of the materials.

(2) As a scholar, Fernando was allowed of only one choice among several options for completing the course.

A Number Of; The Number Of – This expression or phrase *a number of* requires the *plural form* of the verb, while *the number of* needs the *singular* verb in a demonstrative sentence.

Ex. (1) There *are* a number of rotten eggs in the basket.

(2) A number of students *were* present in the rally site.

(3) The number of endangered animals *is* increasing every year.

Apropos – As *adjective* (pronounced minus "s"), this word means *to the point (pertinent)*; as *adverb*, *by the way* or *suitably as regards time or circumstances;* and as *preposition, with reference to*.

Ex. (1) *Adjective*: We are sending this information apropos to your request for clarification.

(2) *Adverb*: The judgment call was done apropos to the protest.

(3) *Preposition*: [in lieu og regarding] Apropos your order, here is our current quotation.

Armed To The Teeth – It is a condition in which *one has all the necessary things or is well- equipped to do something.*

Ex. (1) The platoon of soldiers were <u>armed to the teeth</u> when they came to disperse the demonstrators.

(2) Being <u>armed to the teeth</u> with a doctorate in philosophy, and having an extensive exposure in rural development abroad during a stint with the UNDP, she came home to tackle the poverty problem in the countryside.

Arrive – *Arrive at* means *to reach* a *specific place* or *situation; arrive* without the preposition *at* means *to win success*.

Ex. (1) He <u>arrived at</u> the plaza as expected.

(2) We <u>arrived at</u> a conclusion that she was right.

(3) *Idiomatic*: He has <u>arrived</u> as a businessman. [He is successful.]

As Follows – *As follows* is the correct expression used in enumeration.

Ex. (1) The officers elected are <u>as follows</u>:

(2) (Note: The enumeration follows here.)

Attached Herewith – *Attached herewith* smacks of *redundancy, wordiness* or *superfluity*.

Ex. (1) *Wrong*: <u>Attached herewith </u>is the list of officers.

(2) *Right*: <u>Attached</u> is the list of...

(3) *Right*: <u>Herewith</u> is the list of...

Avail... Of – An *appropriate reflexive pronoun* is always inserted between the verb *avail* and the preposition *of*.

Ex. (1) The man <u>availed *himself* of</u> the new discount on the price of shoes.

(2) The teachers <u>availed *themselves* of</u> the GSIS loan.

(3} <u>Avail *yourself* of</u> this new offer.

Bad As *Adjective After a Linking Verb* – In its use together with linking verbs, *bad* (adjective) and not *badly* (adverb) is the proper form.

Ex. (1) He felt <u>bad.</u>

(2) The food tasted <u>bad</u>.

(3) *Right* (adverb): The sick gourmet tasted badly the adobo.

Bad as *Adverb Is Not Correct – Badly* should be the correct *adverb form.*

Ex.   (1) *Wrong*: His tooth ached so bad he could not sleep.

(2) *Right*: His tooth ached so badly *that* he could not sleep.

(3) *Right*: The contestant fared badly in his quest for victory.

Badly Needed; **B**adly In Need Of – *Badly needed* and *badly in need of* are now good English phrases.

Ex.   (1) The money was badly needed by the farmer.

(2) The building is badly in need of repair.

Bark Up The Wrong Tree; **B**ark At The Moon or **B**ay At The Moon – *Bark up the wrong tree*, not *bark at*, is *to complain to the wrong party*. It must not be confused with *bark at* which means *to bay* or *wail* as the dog faces its enemy or quarry; *bay at the moon* is when a dog *barks at the moon* for reasons known only to it.

Ex.   (1) The farmers barked up the wrong tree when they complained to the governor about the abusive landowners.

(2) The sad mother dog that lost its puppies barked at the moon.

(3) Don't bay at the moon like a puppy.

Because – *Because* is a conjunction indicating *cause* or *reason*. Redundancy must be avoided in its use.

Ex.   (1) *Wrong and redundant*: The reason for his absence was because he was ill.

(2) *Right:* Hermes was absent because he was ill.

(3) *Right*: The reason for his absence was illness.

Beside; **B**esides – *Beside* is a *preposition* that means *near* or *alongside; besides* is an *adverb*

meaning *also, moreover...*

Ex.   (1) He built a cottage beside the old acacia tree.

(2) She is pretty and intelligent, besides being rich.

Between; Among – *Between* is used when speaking of only *two persons or things* and *among*, for *three or more persons or things*.

Ex. (1) She was made to choose <u>between</u> career and marriage.

(2) Pert bought the sports edition <u>among</u> the three new car models.

Between... And... – *Between... and...* not *Between... to...* is correct.

Ex. (1) The waves varied <u>between</u> 5 feet <u>and</u> 10 feet in height.

Bring; Take – *Bring* is a verb used by the *speaker* when he wants a *thing to be placed near him from a distance;* take is used by the *speaker* when he wants a *thing near him to be placed away from him.*

Ex. (1) <u>Bring</u> that book to me.

(2) <u>Bring</u> your finished projects tomorrow.

(3) <u>Take</u> this garbage away.

(4) <u>Take</u> home all your graded outputs for your parents to see.

Bring The House Down – It means *to cause the audience to laugh boisterously loud at his funny antics.*

Ex. (1) The comedian's hilarious antics <u>brought the house down</u>.

Buckle Down – This phrase means t*o get seriously ready to do work.*

Ex. (1) Lisa <u>buckled down</u> to redesign her house.

Call Down – *Call down* is *to invoke* or *to reprimand.*

Ex. (1) Pete <u>called down</u> his rights of membership when he asked for a copy of an audited financial report.

(2) Julius <u>called down</u> Jomarie for being disobedient.

Call In – *Call in* is used *to demand payment of debt* or *to summon for assistance.*

Ex. (1) Fe <u>called in</u> Belinda's help in solving Ardie's problem.

(2) Friendship ends when one <u>calls in</u> the payment of the other's long-time debt.

Call It A Day - This phrase means *to end work or an activity.*

Ex. (1) Let's <u>call it a day</u> as it's already past 5 o'clock p.m.

Call It Quits – This idiom expresses the *end of a deal* with *no one at the losing end.*

Ex. (1) You can <u>call it quits</u> now that nobody is at a disadvantage.

Call On – *Call on* is an idiomatic expression that means *to visit, to appeal,* or *to attract attention.*

Ex. (1) *Visit*: Leny <u>called on</u> her friends.

(2) *Appeal*: The President <u>called on</u> the business sector help in the rehabilitation of the typhoon-ravaged areas.

(2) *Attract attention*: The program director <u>called on</u> the participants to have focus in their acts.

Call The Shots – This idiomatic phrase refers to a *person who has the final say* in an organization.

Ex. (1) Mr. Reyes <u>calls the shots</u> in our department.

Can and **May** – In formal usage, the modal *can* indicates ability *to do something* and the modal *may* expresses permission *to do it; can* signifies *possession of specified power* or *means,* or *skill. May* is used to express or indicate *permission, possibility, obligation,* or *function, desire* or *contingency.*

Ex. (1) *Power*: The President <u>can</u> veto the bills passed by Congress.

(2) *Capability:* He <u>can</u> tune the piano. (<u>Can</u> is *permissible* in some interrogative constructions as in *requests* and *refusals, of requests* in outright negative statements.

Ex. Why <u>can't</u> I have one more banana?)

(3) *Permission:* <u>May</u> I use your phone? Yes, you <u>may</u>.

(Note that most Filipino speakers substitute <u>can</u> for <u>may</u> in the example above.

When *permission* is being sought to use the telephone, <u>can</u> is wrong. Assuming that the telephone is not out of order, one <u>can</u> use it as he has the *ability to operate the device, but propriety dictates that he may not do so without permission* of the house owner. In cases of rules and regulations not explicitly known, <u>can</u> may be used for permission: <u>Can</u> we sit here? <u>Can</u> I park here?)

(4) *Possibility*: It <u>may</u> rain this afternoon.

(5) *Obligation*: Congress may set the date of the elections soon. (When an act is mandated by law, shall is used: Congress shall proclaim the duly elected President.)

(6) *Desire* or *wish*: Long may he live! May the best man win!

(7) *Contingency*: The secretary published the data on income and expenditure of the city government so that the people may know. (Note: The past form of *may* is *might*; for *can*, it is *could*.)

Can Of Worms – This phrase stands for *small pocket of problems*.

Ex. (1) The opening of a can of worms in the purchasing department compounded the manager's woes during the investigation.

Can't Stand – *Can't stand* signifies that one *cannot allow* or *tolerate another's action*.

Ex. (1) Rufa can't stand Cesar's antics, but she did nothing.

(2) The baby sitter left her job as she can't stand the child's tantrums.

Chicken Out – *Chicken out* is a verb phrase that means *to lose courage in pursuing something in the face of a formidable obstacle*.

Ex. (1) Carlo chickened out when he learned that the object of his crush was an honor student.

(2) The rebels chickened out and high-tailed it upon being informed of incoming soldiers armed to the teeth.

Collaborate; Corroborate – *Collaborate* is a verb that means *to work together or cooperate*, while *corroborate* is *to issue a statement supporting another's allegation or pronouncement*.

Ex. (1) The group collaborated with the NGO to assist the victims.

(2) The spy collaborated with the Japanese Kempetai during World War II.

(3) The witness corroborated the statement of the accused.

(4) He submitted evidence to corroborate the testimony of the accused.

Come ... followed by time or date as in "come December 2025" is an *adverbial phrase (adverb of time)*; *come* is not used as a verb, hence, its form is not changed when indicating the *future* time.

Ex. (1) Our national economy will improve come December 2025.

Come To A Head – This phrase means *to meet in a competition* or *to come up in conflict against another.*

Ex. (1) The teams come to a head in their final match tomorrow.

(2) Carlos came to a head with the club president on the project plan.

Committed To – This phrase *committed to* is followed by the noun form of *–ing verb*, or *gerund*.

Ex. (1) The brave and patriotic soldiers are committed to *defending* their country at all costs.

Compare To; Compare With – *Compare to* is used in pointing out differences and *compare with* to indicate similarities.

Ex. (1) Compared to her twin sister, Paula is much more intelligent.

(2) The color orange when compared with red is also very attractive to the baby boy.

Comply With – *Comply with* is correct in the example below. *Comply to* is incorrect. (Do not be confused with *agree with* and *agree to*.)

Ex. (1) You must comply with the law, rules, regulations, memoranda, and/or policies being issued or implemented by the duly constituted authorities.

(2) The measurement shall comply with engineering standards.

Cool – An *all-purpose slang* suggesting a relaxed situation, meaning *OK, good, great, terrific,* etc.

Ex. (1) The new girl next door looks cool.

(2) How do you do? Well, I'm doing cool.

Cope With *Is Correct*; **Cope Up** *Is Wrong* – *Cope* means *to struggle or fight with some degree of success*. It must not be confused with keep up, which means *to get abreast with*, as cope *needs the preposition* with, *and not* up.

Ex. (1) Hernan copes with the demands of his job.

(2) If you cannot cope with your tasks, adopt prioritization without upsetting the timetable needs of the office.

(3) Assumpta keeps up with the demands of art and fashion.

(4) With her meager salary as a teacher, she cannot cope with high prices of basic goods.

Cup of Tea – This phrase means *line of specialty* or *field of work*.

Ex. (1) I did not accept the job; it being not my cup of tea.

Cut And Cut Clean – An imperative, this idiomatic verb phrase is directed to a person that he needs *to disengage himself from a situation, while he has still the upper hand to avoid adverse complications later.*

Ex. (1) At the height of People Power protest in 1986, the then President Marcos was told by an American official to cut and cut clean.

(2) The deep penetration agent successfully cut and cut clean from the drug syndicate

after gathering enough evidence to bust the group.

Cut One's Teeth – This phrase means *to learn and polish one's trade.*

Ex. (1) Monina cut her teeth as a journalist while working with the *Iloilo Times.*

Despite; In Spite Of – *Despite*, like *in spite of,* is a *preposition* which means *notwithstanding* or *regardless of. Despite* needs *no preposition* after it.

Ex. (1) The tribal chief was convicted despite his innocence

(2) Tirso ran for mayor in spite of his meager financial resources.

Differ With; Differ From – *Differ with* a person and *differ from* another in certain aspects are correct usage. *Differ than* is wrong.

Ex. (1) Willy differed with Sammy on the proposal.

(2) Grace differs from Mercy in character.

Down In The Mouth – A condition of a person *saddened or made sorry by a situation involving another or himself.*

Ex. (1) Ven was *down in the mouth* to say much on what happened to Luisito.

Due To – *Due to* is an *adjective* used as a complement of the state-of-being verb (to be) like *am, is, are, was,* or *were* (linking verb), meaning *attributable* or *owing to.* It is wrong to use *due to* in place of the conjunction *because.*

Ex. (1) *Bad English*: The soldier ran amok <u>due to</u> serious personal problems.

(2) *Right:* He ran amok <u>because</u> of serious personal problems.

(3) *Right*: The soldier's act of running amuck *was* <u>due to</u> his serious personal problems.

(4) The extensive building damage *was* <u>due to</u> tsunami.

(5) His success *is* <u>due to</u> his diligence.

(6) Oliver was admitted to the Academy <u>owing to</u> hard work. .

<u>Elbow One's Way</u> – *To force one's access or entry in a difficult situation* is the meaning of this phrase.

Ex. (1) Piolo <u>elbowed his way</u> through the crowd to interview the President.

<u>Equate</u>…<u>With</u>…– *Equate with* (not *equalize*) is the correct expression used in comparison of almost equal abilities.

Ex. (1) The war analyst <u>equated</u> the foxiness of Erwin <u>with</u> the cunning of Douglas.

<u>Every Day; Everyday</u> – The expression *every day* (two words) is an *adverb*. *Everyday* (one word) is an *adjective*.

Ex. (1) Adv: The prince visits the estate <u>every day</u>. (Adverb: *Every day* modifies *visits.)*

(2) Adv: We go to school <u>every day</u>.

(3) Adj: Bad weather is an <u>everyday</u> occurrence near the isolated island.

<u>Eyeball To Eyeball</u> – This phrase means *close and direct confrontation.*

Ex. (1) The two gang leaders had an <u>eyeball to eyeball</u> challenge before the gang fight started.

<u>Fall Foul Of</u> – *Fall foul of* means *to come to collision with something.*

Ex. (1) The ignorant man <u>falls foul of</u> the law in the city.

<u>Fewer; Less</u> – *Fewer* is used in comparing things that can be counted and *less* for things that cannot be counted.

Ex. (1) There were <u>fewer</u> boys than girls in the library.

(2) <u>Less</u> clouds appear on the horizon today.

F<u>ill In</u>; <u>Fill Out</u> – *Fill in* means *to complete the blanked portions of documents;* while *fill out* is *to complete a document* or *enlarge it to a certain appropriate limit.*

Ex. (1) <u>Fill in</u> all the needed entries in the document.

(2) <u>Fill in</u> the blanks in this test paper with the correct answers.

(3) The petition for change of name must be <u>filled out</u> by a lawyer.

(4) <u>Fill out</u> these empty balloons before the buyer comes.

<u>F</u><u>irst Come, First Served</u> – This expression *first come, first served* is the contracted form of *The first to come is the first to be served.*

Ex. (1) *Wrong*: Come on time; <u>first come first serve</u>.

(2) *Correct*: Take a number; you will be attended to on a <u>first come, first served</u> basis.

<u>F</u><u>oul Play</u> – This expression signifies *criminal violence*. In sports, it is *playing against the rules.*

Ex.   (1) The police left no stone unturned to find out if there was <u>foul play</u> behind his death.

(2) Bob was guilty of a <u>foul play</u> and was recommended for expulsion from the team.

<u>F</u><u>ull-Fledged</u> – The adjective *full-fledged* refers to birds *having all grown or matured feathers.*

Figuratively, *fully* or *completely qualified* if used to describe persons; a semi-skilled person is like a *fledgeling* or *fledgling,* *meaning* a bird that has grown feathers, but not yet ready for flight, hence *immature.*

Ex.   (1) From Associate Professor he was promoted to <u>full-fledged</u> Professor.

(2) The rank of Police Senior Superintendent is equivalent to the rank of <u>full-fledged</u> Colonel in the Army.

(3) The Chief of Staff of the Armed Forces of the Philippines is a <u>full-fledged</u> General

who has four stars to symbolize his rank, like the Director General of the Philippine National Police.

Get The Ball Rolling – *To start the operation going or the system moving* is the meaning of this phrase.

Ex. (1) The crew got the ball rolling immediately and put out in no time the oil rig fire.

(2) "All right, let's get the ball rolling to solve the problem," the professor intoned.

Give One The Air – *To give one the air* means *to dismiss him* or *make one go away*.

Ex. (1) After getting fed up with his antics, Francis gave Warren the air.

Go Easy On – This phrase means *to forego applying sanction or penalty on a person who has committed an infraction of some laws, rules or regulations*.

Ex. (1) The police were told to go easy on the suspect who was the son of a powerful politician.

Go The Extra Mile – *To double one's exertion of efforts to achieve a purpose* means *to go the extra mile*.

Ex. (1) Brian went the extra mile to win the heart of Julie.

(2) For going the extra mile often, Franco succeeded in realizing his dreams.

Grin And Bear It – This phrase means *to reluctantly accept something not desired and suffer its consequence in silence*.

Ex. (1) Bobby had no choice but to accept Myra's decision with a grin and bear it attitude.

Haul Up Before – *To bring to trial before the court* is the meaning of this phrase.

Ex. (1) The suspect in the crime was hauled up before the court by responding lawmen.

Hit It Off – This phrase means *to get on well together*.

Ex. (1) Cynthia and Mark hit it off at their first meeting.

Hit Pay Dirt – *Earn or obtain a lot of money*. *Pay dirt* means *earth or soil containing lode in mines*. Thus, when miners hit pay dirt, it is good fortune for them.

Ex. (1) The writer hit pay dirt at last with the publication of his book, a best seller.

(2) The self-made salesman didn't give up until he had hit pay dirt.

Hit The Nail Right On The Head – This phrase means *to make the correct approach to do efficiently and effectively something that ensures accomplishment.*

Ex. (1) The student hit the nail right on the head so that the teacher required no further explanation.

(2) Hernando always hits the nail right on the head as a very successful entrepreneur.

Hold Water – This refers to *remarks or opinions that have basis in truth or in fact.*

Ex. (1) The pronouncement of Joseph does not hold water, so that he failed to convince the group on the soundness of his proposal.

Hope and the *Present Form of the Verb* – Hope is used with the *present form of the verb* signifying a *positive situation.*

Ex. (1) I hope you *enjoy* the party.

(2) With modal *can*: It is hoped that you *can do* this job as well as you did the other one.

Hope and the *Future Form of the Verb* – Hope is used with *will* plus the *main verb* signifying a *positive* stance.

Ex. (1) We hope they will win.

Hot Water – *Hot water* stands for *trouble.*

Ex. (1) Jose is in hot water for disturbing peace in the plaza.

Imply; Infer - *Imply* is synonymous to *suggest, purport, or hint; to infer* means *to deduce* or *to draw* a conclusion *from.*

Ex. (1) His statement implies that he opposes land reform.

(2) It may be inferred from the senator's reaction that he would vote against the proposed bill.

In Accordance With; In Accord With – *In accordance with,* not *to,* or *in accordance with* which means *in agreement with,* but *according to* when citing sources of information.

Ex. (1) I will sing <u>in accordance with</u> her wishes.

(2) He will be home soon <u>according to</u> his son.

In Cahoots – *In partnership, particularly in shady deals* is the meaning of this phrase.

Ex. (1) The thief was <u>in cahoots</u> with the guard of the factory.

Incredible; Incredulous – *Incredible* is an adjective *to describe something that has no credibility,* or it is a tale *hard to believe. Incredulous* is an adjective that *refers to a person who is skeptical or cannot believe in what he hears.*

Ex. (1) The alleged miracle was very <u>incredible</u>.

(2) Cesar was <u>incredulous</u> when told that Danton survived unscathed during the attack by the crazed man.

In The Family Way – This phrase denotes *a condition of being pregnant.* The correct preposition is *in* not *on.* It must not be confused with *on the way,* which means *an action in progress.*

Ex. (1) "At last, I'm <u>in the family way!</u>" exclaimed Ella, the fortyish wife of Dante after the doctor informed the couple of her pregnancy.

(2) Correct: He is <u>on the way</u> to our meeting when my friend learned of the good news thru a phone text message.

Iron Fist – A strong and decisive action is suggested by this phrase.

Ex. (1) The army general found it necessary to use an <u>iron fist</u> to deal with the rebellious soldiers.

It's Time; It Is High Time – *It's time; it is high time*: these two expressions *always require verbs in the past tense.*

Ex. (1) <u>It's time</u> the police *arrested* the thief who had victimized several households in the district.

(2) <u>It's high time</u> we *did* something to stem the tide of immorality.

Jibe With – *Jibe with* means *to fit in with. Jive* is a slang meaning *phony, often connected with jazz.*

Ex. (1) His airs did not <u>jibe with</u> the idiosyncrasy of the group.

Keep One's Cool – This phrase means *stay* or *remain calm despite being exposed to a tight or unpleasant situation.*

Ex. (1) Manuel kept his cool despite the insulting taunt of Vir.

Keep and **For Keeps** – *Keep* is a noun that *suggests personal support or maintenance for living*, while *for keeps* means *something received that is not to be returned*.

Ex. (1) The lazy man begs for his keep.

(2) That car is yours for keeps.

Keep One's Head Above Water – This phrase means *to stay out of financial difficulties*.

Ex. (1) The teachers could hardly keep their heads above water; they can't cope with the high cost of living owing to low salaries.

Keep Under Wraps – *To hide or be secretive about a certain act* is the meaning of this phrase.

Ex. (1) Upon orders of his boss, Wilfredo kept under wraps the anomalous transactions of Luis that he discovered.

Keep One's Score – This phrase means *to maintain excellence*.

Ex. (1) Despite his penury, he kept his score and completed the course with flying colors.

Knee Jerk – It is *a sudden reactive impulse or action that is not usually sustained*.

Ex. (1) Most politicians assume a knee jerk stance in dealing with problems affecting their constituents after hearing much criticisms from several sectors of society.

Lay and **Lie** – *Lay* is a transitive verb meaning *to place*, while *lie* which means *to recline* is intransitive (it takes no object). The past tense of *lay* is *laid*, while *lie* has *lay* for its past form.

Lie is usually followed by *down*.

Ex. (1) The ambassadors usually lay wreaths at the Rizal Shrine as a matter of cultural courtesy.

(2) The scouts were made to lie awake long into the night to observe sounds of night animals.

(3) As soon as Sheila arrived home she laid her things on the floor and lay down beside them.

(4) Kaya lay down on the cushion pad that she laid on the table and slept to the consternation of the maid. Note: In Ex. (3) *laid* is the past form of *lay* (*to place*); *lay* is the past form of *lie* meaning *to recline*. *Lied* is the past form of *lie*, which means *to make false statement or information*.

Lay Bare – This phrase means *to reveal something being kept to oneself*.

Ex.   (1) The leader of the prisoners laid bare his escape plans for the group.

Lay Down The Law – *To speak with authority* is a phrase attributed to a person who *exercises management power over* a group.

Ex.   (1) Jimmy as the supervisor always lays down the law and his men are happy in their work.

Lay One's Card On The Table – *To express one's views on an issue without reservation* is the meaning of this phrase.

Ex.   (1) Rico laid his cards on the table and made everybody support his win-win solution to the issue.

Lay One Under An Obligation – This phrase means *to be able to convince another to do him or others a favor*.

Ex.   (1) Pol laid all the group members under an obligation.

Lay Oneself Open To – It is a situation in which one is compelled *to expose oneself to criticism*.

Ex.   (1) After announcing his candidacy, he laid his personal life open to all comments and criticisms from his neighbors.

Lay On The Table – *To put something aside to be acted on later*, as an activity that has lower priority than others.

Ex. (1) The presiding officer had the proposal laid on the table.

Lay Up For The Rainy Day – *To save money for the future* is the meaning of this phrase.

Ex. (1) Gorgonio laid up a hefty sum for the rainy day.

Leave In The Cold – This phrase means to *abandon someone*.

Ex. (1) The reneging boyfriend left his fiancee in the cold.

Leave No Stone Unturned – This is an idiomatic expression meaning *to do everything necessary in discovering the truth.*

Ex. (1) The investigator left no stone unturned in establishing the truth on what happened.

Leg To Stand On – That *one's contention has* factual or *legal basis* is the meaning this phrase.

Ex. (1) The defense lawyer countered that the argument of the prosecution has no leg to stand on, for the latter cited the law that is not applicable to the case at bar.

Leg Room – *A sufficient leeway or allowance for action* is suggested by this phrase.

Ex. (1) The commanding general gave his field commanders wider leg room to implement peace initiatives with the rebels.

Lend A Hand – This expression means *to give help in doing something.*

Ex. (1) Alexis lent a hand to Sigfred in doing his project.

Let Alone – *Let alone* may be used in place of *leave out* or *not consider.*

Ex. (1) Andrew let alone the suggestion of Dick.

Let In ... On – Allow another to know what to what has been agreed on or planned by other persons.

Ex. Cynthia let in Karen on their secret plan to sell RTW's to their co-employees.

Let On – *Let on* is an *idiomatic expression* meaning *to allow another to know something he has no idea about.*

Ex. (1) Dave let on Eli in the secret agreement he made with the group.

Let One's Guard Down – *To be lax and complacent in his watch.*

Ex. (1) Arvin was cornered by his enemy when he let his guard down.

Let Out; Let The Cat Out The Bag - The phrase *let out* means *to release from confinement.* To let the cat out of the bag is similar to *spill the beans.*

Ex. (1) Cindy let the bird out of the cage.

(2) The confession of the suspect let the cat out of the bag.

Let Up – This phrase is a verb meaning *to stop* and a noun, which is *cessation of an activity*.

Ex. (1) The rains let up for a few minutes and poured again.

(2) There was no let up in their campaign against pornography.

Line One's Pockets – *To misappropriate amounts of money that does not belong to him* is the meaning of this phrase.

Ex. (1) The corrupt politician lined up his pockets in order to win another term of office.

Majority Of – *As idiom* this phrase needs the article *the*.

Ex. (1) *Wrong*: Majority of the teachers stopped developing.

(2) *Right*: The majority of the teachers stopped developing.

(3) *Right*: Most of the teachers stopped developing.

Make A Clean Breast Of – This verb phrase means *to open up pent emotions of disappointment*.

Ex. (1) Facing the inevitable, Cesar made a clean breast of the doubts and suspicions he had against his superior officer.

Make Eyes At – *Make eyes at* means *to try to attract the attention of a girl*.

Ex. (1) Philip made eyes at Trixia but she failed to notice him.

Make Waves – *To attract attention after doing something* is to *make waves*.

Ex. (1) The beautiful girl made waves at the mall by parading around in a flimsy bikini.

Make the Cut – *Pass the standard set* is the meaning of this phrase; it is similar in meaning to *fit to a tee*.

Ex. (1) The girl's father said that her suitor does not make the cut.

Maybe – *Maybe* (one word) is an *adverb*.

Ex. (1) Maybe he would be late today.

May Be – *May be* is a verb phrase indicating a *possibility of something to happen*. *May* is a modal helping the verb *be* (main verb).

Ex. (1) Hernando may be late today.

Might - *Might* signifies *obligation* in sentences *containing mild reproof.* The other use of *might* is the past form of *may.*

Ex. (1) *Reproof:* You might show some gratitude.

(2) *Past form of may:* She might win as mayor, who knows?

Must - *Must* is another *auxiliary* (modal) that indicates *necessity of complying with* an *obligation*

or a *need* called for by the circumstances.

Ex. (1) You must go home now.

Nevertheless – *Nevertheless* is an *adverb* like *notwithstanding.*

Ex. (1) June was late; nevertheless, she made it to the program and sang very well.

Notwithstanding - *Notwithstanding* is a *preposition* that means *in spite of, regardless of;* an *adverb* like *nevertheless, all the same* and *conjunction* meaning *although.*

Ex. (1) *Preposition:* Cosme married Petra notwithstanding the opposition of his family.

(2) *Adverb:* The big boat capsized in the violent waves, notwithstanding.

(3) *Conjunction:* He reported, notwithstanding he was ill.

Note: *Notwithstanding* indicates weakest opposition, while *despite* is relatively stronger than *notwithstanding,* and *in spite of* reflects opposition most active and most vigorous.

One Of - This phrase *one of,* usually followed by the article *the* (except when a pronoun follows

it, as in *one of you*), is always followed by a *plural noun.* This *one of the* phrase, followed by a *plural noun* when used as *subject of the sentence, requires a singular verb.* The actual subject is the pronoun *one.*

Ex. (1) One of the *speakers* in the celebration *is* President Gloria Macapagal Arroyo.

(2) One of the *boys appears* very famished.

(3) Perla is one of the *girls* who *sing* off-key.

(4) *Correct* (no *one of* phrase used as subject): Perla is one *girl* who <u>sings</u> off-key.

Note: In Ex.(1)and(2) the singular pronoun <u>one</u> in the *one of* phrase is the subject of the sentence to which the verb *is* and *appears*, respectively, agrees with. In

Ex.(3) the subject of the sentence is *Perla*, and the linking verb <u>is</u> agrees with it, whereas the referent of the relative pronoun *who* in the *who clause* is *girls* to which the verb <u>sing</u> agrees with.

Only – *Only* is both an a*dverb* and a *conjunction*.

Ex.   (1) *Conjunction*: They would have come <u>only</u> the car broke down.(*Only*, equivalent of *but*).

(2) *Adverb*: He arrived <u>only</u> an hour ago

(3) Bert recognizes not <u>only</u> the legal *but* also the moral issue.

(4) Dictators respect <u>only</u> force.

(5) I <u>only</u> work here.   (He does not reside but only work in the place.)

(6) <u>Only</u> I work here.   (He is the lone worker in the area.)

(7) I work here <u>only</u>.   (He works in the area, not elsewhere.)

On The Road – This prepositional phrase suggests *a situation in progress of traveling or movement*. As *adverb* it indicates *some place other than the residence of a group*.

Ex.   (1) While <u>on the road</u> to Boracay, we stopped at Altavas to rest.

(2) The community is now <u>on the road</u> toward lasting peace.

(3) The team won three games successively <u>on the road</u>.

On The Street or **On** *Plus the Name of the* Street – When indicating location or address the preposition *on*, <u>not</u> *in, plus the name of the street* is used.

Ex.   (1) Mr. Librodo's office is <u>on Ledesma St</u>., Iloilo City.

      (2) A big shopping mall stands <u>on Benigno Aquino Avenue</u>.

Note: <u>In the street</u> or *in* plus *the name of the street* is used to refer to a location *actually astride the street,* thus:

Ex.(1) The Ati-atihan group dances in the street.

Ex.(2) The vehicular collision happened in Quezon Street.

Operate On; Operate – *Operate on* means *to cut up anatomically* or *to remove dead or damaged portion of a body,* especially human body. *Operate* means *to make a machine run* or *manipulate the controls to make motorized gadgets function.*

Ex. (1) The surgeon operated on the patient for two hours.

(2) The test car driver operates any machine he likes.

Pain In The Neck – This is a noun referring to *a person who poses behavioral or disciplinary problem to one who has moral ascendancy over him.*

Ex. (1) Carlo is a pain in the neck to his grandmother who takes care of him.

Paint The Town Red – *To go about the place and enjoy partying or drinking spirits* is the meaning of this phrase.

Ex. (1) Rex invited Jimmy to his birthday bash in a club and they painted the town red.

Paper Over – *To hide* or *minimize the ill-effects of* an untoward incident means *to paper over.*

Ex. (1) The drumbeaters of the administration promptly papered over the incident as an isolated one.

Participate In - *Participate* needs the preposition *in*.

Ex. (1) The Girl Scouts participated in the athletic meet.

(2) The program was participated in by the Freshmen.

Pat In The Back – A friendly recognition and encouragement for something good done by a person is a pat in the back.

Ex. (1) The principal gave Reynaldo a pat in the back for his very effective teaching.

People; Person – *People* is used for *a large group in round numbers of persons* and *person* for *exact number or smaller group of individuals.*

Ex.(1) People massed in the plaza to listen to foreign guests.

(2) The food was prepared for twenty persons.

Play By The Rules – *To observe* and *follow man-made and natural laws or course of things* means *to play by the rules*.

Ex. (1) Success is sweet when accomplished on morally high grounds by the achiever who <u>played by the rules</u>.

(2) <u>Play by the rules</u> and you'll go a long way in serving your constituents

Play On – *To exploit* or *to take advantage of* another is *to play on him*.

Ex. (1) Imelda <u>played on</u> Karen's innocence by selling her a cheap article at an exorbitant price.

Prefer… To… - The transitive verb *prefer* always needs the preposition *to* when there are only two options to choose from.

Ex. (1) "I <u>prefer</u> the Philippines run like hell by the Filipinos <u>to</u> the Philippines run like heaven by the Americans."

(2) The manager <u>preferred</u> Silvio's marketing proposal <u>to</u> Oscar's.

Presently – *Presently* is an adverb that means *soon* and <u>not</u> *now*. *At present* is the correct phrase when one means *now*.

Ex. (1) President Arroyo said that the Iloilo flood control project will be constructed <u>presently</u>.

Press One's Luck – *To insist on pursuing bigger stakes after winning smaller ones* is the meaning of this phrase.

Ex. (1) The inveterate gambler continued on <u>pressing his luck</u> and lost every penny he had.

Pride Himself On; Take Pride In – This phrase *to pride himself on* means to show or strut off one's acquisition; *to take pride in a deed or feat done* is to show elation over one's success.

Ex. (1) Hero <u>prided himself on</u> the fact that he owns the latest model of Mercedes Benz sports car.

(2) The indigent girl <u>took pride in</u> her being valedictorian of her class.

Pull One's Leg – *To play a trick on or dupe another person* is the meaning of this phrase.

Ex. (1) Victor <u>pulled Sancho's leg</u> when he told the latter that he won in the lotto draw.

Pull One's Punches – This phrase signifies a second-thought action *to go easy on the use of power or authority against a recalcitrant or suspected violators of the law.*

Ex.   (1) The governor pulled his punches when a relative was involved in the shady transaction being investigated.

Pull The Wool Over One's Eyes – *To hide the truth by dubious means* is the meaning of this phrase.

Ex.   (1) It was so easy for a seasoned politician like him to pull the wool over his constituents' eyes.

Put Away – *To put away* is correct, not *to keep in order scattered belongings or dishes.*

Ex.   (1) Put away your toys that are scattered on the floor.

Put Off – Put off means *to defer* or *to postpone* an activity.

Ex.   (1) The committee put off the discussion on the matter in question.

Put One's Best Foot Forward – Despite the fact that man has only two feet, *to do his best performance* is to put his best foot forward.

Ex.   (1) The coach advised every man in the team to put his best foot forward.

Put One's Foot Down – To put one's foot down means *to disapprove something proposed or suggested to him.*

Ex.   (1) The commander put his foot down when his captain made a suggestion.

Put One Over – *To have the upper hand over someone's act* is to *put one over* him.

Ex.   (1) Efren put one over Nick's bluff.

Put Up With – This expression means *to endure without resentment.*

Ex.   (1) The nanny put up with her ward's tantrum.

(2) The debater of the affirmative side valiantly put up with his counterpart on the negative side.

Raring To Go – This phrase means *very eager to go.*

Ex. (1) The kids are raring to go to the carnival.

Regardless – *Regardless,* never *irregardless,* is correct as te latter is not good English and *not be used* even in informal way.

Ex. (1) Ramiro sailed for Masbate regardless of the turbulent sea.

Rein In – To *rein in* means *to exercise absolute control* over one's group.

Ex. (1) The bandit leader reined in some of his rebellious men by threatening to kill members of the latter's families.

Renege On – *Renege on* signifies *to break* a *promise* or *fail to comply with an obligation.*

Ex. (1) He reneged on his promise to marry her.

Run Across – This phrase means *to meet by chance.*

Ex. (1) Ness Janine ran across a long lost friend at the mall.

(2) The unsuspecting rangers ran across a group of illegal loggers.

(3) The examinees had no inkling that they would run across vague questions, hence they were greatly disappointed.

Run Into – *Run into* signifies *to collide with unintentionally or met by accident* or *to get into a state or condition.* *Run into* may be used also to express effect of some big event.

Ex. (1) Russell ran into Jimmy and angered the latter; but after their dagger's looks at each other, it dawned on them that they were long lost old friends.

(2) The damage of the South Asian tsunami runs into billions of dollars.

See Eye To Eye – *To agree* is the meaning of this phrase.

Ex. (1) Rina and Excelsa always see eye to eye in their relationship as friends.

See To It – *See to it* is followed by the conjunction *that.*

Ex. (1) The teacher always sees to it *that* the students do their part.

Set A Store By – This expression means *to put a high value on* one's *expectations* of another person.

Ex.   (1) Mang Ramon <u>sets a store by</u> his youngest son who is a brilliant student.

<u>Set One's Face Against</u> – *To resist strongly* is the meaning of this phrase.

Ex.   (1) The floor leader <u>set his face against</u> any amendment to his bill during the hearing yesterday.

<u>Set People By The Ears</u> – This phrase means *to stir up trouble.*

Ex.   (1) The rebel leader tried hard to <u>set people by the ears</u> as the Army group continues to win back the rural folk from their influence.

<u>Set The Tone</u> – *To start the way in doing things as he wishes* is to *set the tone.*

Ex.   (1) Fely <u>set the tone</u> in the activity of her group.

<u>Shall</u> and <u>Will</u> – The use of another pair of modal, *shall* and *will,* presents some difficulty. In the

first person shall <u>is not emphatic *and* does not impose obligation</u>, but *in the second and third*

persons, shall is used <u>emphatically and with obligation being imposed</u>. *Will* <u>is emphatic only</u>

when used in the *first person.*

Ex.   (1) *Without assurance of complying with or doing what one promises:* I <u>shall</u> return.

(2) *Emphatic and with self-imposed obligation:* I <u>will</u> defend your right to express your

opinion, although I may not agree with you.

(3) *With imposition, or sanction by rule or by law:* You or Hernan <u>shall</u> be liable for the

loss of the tools.

(4) *Liability by Contract:* You <u>shall</u> pay your account or your mortgaged property <u>will</u> be foreclosed (or taken over) by the bank.

(5) *Direction without obligation to comply with or obey strictly:* You <u>will</u> see him in the morning as soon as you have time.

(6) *Without obligation:* He <u>will</u> do it on his own time.

(7) *With obligation as sanctioned by law.* You shall play by the rules or face the full force of the law.

Share... With; Share In – *Share with* means *to share* a thing *with* a person, while *share in*

signifies *to share in* something.

Ex.(1) He shared the bread with his sisters.

(2) The members of the cooperative shared in the year-end profits.

Shed or Cast Off – To *shed* or *cast off* is correct, but *shed off* is wrong.

Ex.   (1) He sheds his real self in his dramatic role.

(2) The snake cast off its skin. The snake shed its skin.

Shot In The Arm – *A much-needed concrete encouragement or support given to a slowing or*

decadent activity is implied by this phrase.

Ex.   (1) The mayor gave the task force a much needed shot in the arm with sufficient budget and

additional personnel.

Slow – *Slow* as *adverb* is now accepted.

Ex.   (1) Drive slow!

Smattering – *Smattering* means *slight knowledge*.

Ex.   (1) Jamie has a smattering knowledge of geology.

(2) Theda speaks Tagalog with a smattering of Ilonggo.

So... That ... - *So* is followed by an adjective which precedes *that*.

Ex.   (1) Mrs. Mindanao was so nervous that every time she speaks she stammered.

Spatter; Sputter – To *spatter* means *to project drops of fluid onto or to fall in drops; to sputter* is

to resemble a small explosion of sudden sounds.

Ex.   (1) The speeding car spattered mud onto the pedestrians.

(2) The airplane sputtered and crashed into the water.

Spill The Beans – This is an idiomatic expression that means *to reveal the truth* or *information* behind the scene.

Ex. (1) When cornered by the lawyer, the witness spilled the beans to the jurors.

Square Off – This phrase means *to make up for some failings* or *avenge a loss*.

Ex. (1) Nerio had to square off his debts or he will lose his friend.

(2) Nida squared off her grudges with Cielito by peaceful talk.

Square Shooter – An *honest person* who is also fair and square in his dealings.

Ex. (1) The square shooter handily won over the wheeler-dealer in a fair and square deal.

Stand Ground – This phrase means *to stand pat* or *hold on to a territorial position* or *to stay put*.

An appropriate pronoun is placed between *stand* and *ground*.

Ex. (1) The striking employees stood *their* ground despite the rumbling water tankers and

armed soldiers coming to disperse them.

(2) Liberty was compelled to stand *her* ground on the issue of granting too much freedom

to her growing children as suggested by her mother-in-law.

Stir Up A Hornet's Nest – This idiom means *to arouse the fierce anger of a number of people*.

Ex. (1) The advisers of the President were afraid to stir up a hornet's nest among Poe's fans,

so that they discouraged the Department of Justice from filing cases of sedition

against the fiery speakers during the eulogy to the "King of Philippine Movies."

Such... A – *Such* followed by a *singular noun* requires the article *a* before the noun.

Ex.   (1) The setting up of such a *facility* will increase employment in the area.

Such... As – *Such* is followed by a noun preceding *as*.

Ex.   (1) We will wait until such time as the boat is ready.

Such A... That -- *Such a* plus *that* is used as follows:

Ex.   (1) She was in such a hurry that she failed to switch off the flatiron which started the fire.

Sweep One Off His Feet – This phrase means *to have someone totally attracted to, smitten by or*

enamored of him.

Ex.   (1) She was so gorgeous that Celino was swept off his feet by her.

Tail – When used as a verb it means *to follow someone and observe his actions,* usually, without

his knowledge.

Ex.   (1) Mario *tailed* Freddie to find out if he works for the syndicate.

Tailgate – To *tailgate* is *to drive dangerously close* following another vehicle.

Ex.   (1) Bonifacio keeps on tailgating as he drives thru the city and endangers himself and the

passengers of the other car.

Take Aback – This phrase means *to feel or experience small unpleasant shock* resulting from

observation.

Ex.   (1) Gloria was taken aback by his brazen lie.

Take Advice To, *not* At – Care must be observed in the use of *prepositions* with the expression

take advice.

Ex. (1) *Wrong*: She took advice at heart.

(2) *Right*: ... took advice to heart.

Take After – Take after means *to inherit the traits or physical features of a parent.*

Ex. (1) Cristina took after her mother's beautiful body.

Take Care Of – In this phrase *care* is a noun, *take*, being the verb, assumes the *past* or *present*

tense form or *any other forms* of the verb as the case may be.

Ex. (1) Everything was taken care of.

(2) Ellen Mae took care of her baby brother when her mother became an overseas

Filipino worker.

Take For A Ride – This phrase means *to deceive or fool or cheat*

someone.

Ex. (1) Sergio took Martin for a ride and cheated him of several thousand pesos.

(2) Be smart; do not allow someone to take you for a ride by being gullible.

Take It On The Chin – The meaning of this phrase is *to endure punishment or misfortune*

without complaining.

Ex. (1) Gerry took it on the chin when he was imprisoned for an offense he did not commit.

Take The Bull By The Horns – *To tackle directly or head-on a formidable problem* is one

meaning of this phrase.

Ex. (1) Jerry took the bull by the horns and successfully hurdled the test.

Take To – *Take to* means *to develop* a *fondness, aptitude* or *liking* for certain way *of doing*

things.

Ex.   (1) Being a happy person, Isidro took to dancing in no time at all.

Take To Task – *To criticize another's action* is the meaning of take to task.

Ex.   (1) The politician was taken to task by a commentator.

Take Up The Cudgels – Taking up the cudgels means *to defend strongly in an argument a fellow*

or *to continue a weakening advocacy of a cause started by a friend.*

Ex.   (1) A new leader took up the cudgels for the fallen comrade.

(2) His brother did not take up the cudgels for him against their father's contention.

Talk At – *Talk at* is used for *great number of listeners.*

Ex.   (1) We are constantly talked at by teachers, preachers, salesmen, public officials and

moving picture sound tracks.

(2) The scientist talks at a consultation meeting of the citizens.

Talk... Out... - *Talk out* means to *dissuade* or *to discourage* one *from doing* a thing. An

appropriate noun or pronoun is inserted between *talk* and *out* followed by the preposition *of.*

Ex.   (1) Greg was able to talk Rina out of committing suicide.

(2) His mother talked him out of joining the fraternity.

That, *not* Where or When -- *That* and not *where* or *when* is correct *to point out place or time.*

Ex.   (1) It was in Cebu that Jose met Josefa.

(2) It was in June that he won in the lottery.

The Same – *The same* is an adjective. This phrase functions as a *noun* when *used alone* without the noun.

Ex. (1) Fria suffered from some form of depression and <u>the same</u> happened to Kisha later.

(2) *Wrong*: Thanks for the book; I'll return <u>same</u> tomorrow.

(*Same* is not accepted in formal usage to take the place of *the same*.)

(3) *Right*: … I'll return <u>the same</u> tomorrow.

<u>T</u>hrow The Book At – *To apply, enforce or to use the full force of the law strictly or to the letter*

to a violator is the meaning of this phrase.

Ex. (1) The fuming police chief <u>threw the book at</u> the recidivist.

<u>T</u>humbs Up – This phrase indicates a *sign of approval.*

Ex. (1) The supervisor gave Rolando his <u>thumbs up</u> for swift and effective action.

<u>T</u>oe The Line – *To toe the line* is the same as *to dance with the music,* which means *to conform*

to or follow the wishes of others against his own.

Ex. (1) Ian has to <u>toe the line</u> to be accepted in the group.

<u>T</u>o Date – *To date* when used does not need *yet*. The adverb *yet* is used alone like the adverbial

expression *to date*.

Ex. (1) *Wrong*: <u>To date</u> nothing has been done <u>yet</u> to correct the situation. (*To date* signifies

the same meaning as *<u>yet</u>*.)

(2) *Right*: <u>To date</u> nothing has been done to correct the anomalous situation.

(3) Nothing has been done <u>yet</u> to correct the situation.

<u>T</u>ooth And Nail – This idiom means *to work hard or laboriously.*

Ex. (1) The farming couple tilled <u>tooth and nail</u> their land to send their children to school.

To Whom – *To whom* and not *from whom* is correct.

Ex. (1) She refused to serve with the group <u>to whom</u> she owes nothing.

Turn Tail – This phrase means *to leave or backtrack, usually discouraged or in fear.*

Ex. (1) The boisterous pranksters <u>turned tail</u> upon noticing burly men approaching them.

(2) The cowardly rebels <u>turned tail</u> on the first volley of fire from the police.

Turn Turtle – *Turn turtle* means *to turn over on its backside.*

Ex. (1) The speeding car <u>turned turtle</u> as it rounded the curve.

Up For Grabs – This phrase suggests *something highly saleable or desirable being dangled for*

   use or benefit of consumers.

Ex. (1) New stocks of gift and novelty articles are <u>up for grabs</u> at the mall.

(2) Valuable prizes are <u>up for grabs</u> in the Dinagyang contest this week.

Up In The Air – To be *up in the air* is to become *undecided on what to do.*

Ex. (1) Greg was <u>up in the air</u> on his running for reelection as president of the club.

Very – *Very* and not *much* is correct here.

Ex. (1) *Wrong*: Teach the students along lines which are <u>much</u> responsive to their present

      need.

   Right: . . . <u>*very*</u> responsive to …

   Right: . . . *much more* responsive. . . .

Wag One's Tongue – *To deliver words of censure in a chattering manner* is the meaning of this phrase.

Ex. (1) His spinster aunt always <u>wags her tongue</u>, but Sim simply ignored her.

<u>W</u>alk On Air – This phrase means *to become light-headed with happiness.*

Ex. (1) Jamby <u>walked on air</u> after winning the beauty contest.

<u>Walk the Talk</u> – *To do what one could perform* or *put a plan into action.*

Ex. (1) After their meeting, the chairperson made the members decide to <u>walk the talk.</u>

(2) "Son, your father would be glad if you could walk the talk," his mother told him.

<u>W</u>ash … Hands Off – This is an *idiomatic expression* that means *to disclaim responsibility* a la

Pontius Pilate. An appropriate pronoun is inserted between *wash* and *hands.*

Ex. (1) The erring employee <u>washed *his* hands off</u> the mess when confronted.

<u>W</u>ater Down – *Water down* is an *idiom* that means *to make criticism less forceful by adding*

remarks intended to mollify or *assuage ruffled feelings.*

Ex. (1) The commentator <u>watered down</u> his vitriolic attacks against a politician after he was

bribed.

(2) To <u>water down</u> his remarks, Pio said, "I daresay you are wrong, but I am not also

right in denouncing you without proof of your wrongdoing."

<u>W</u>ax – An intransitive verb, *wax* is used in rhetorical sense meaning *to grow* or *to become.*

Ex. (1) The rising moon <u>waxed</u> silvery.

(2) Cecilia used to <u>wax</u> eloquently oratorical, so that she was elected municipal councilor with the highest number of votes.

Who; **Whom** – If a *relative pronoun* serves as the *subject of the subordinate clause, who* or

whoever is correct; if *object within the subordinate clause, whom* or *whomever* is used.

Ex.   (1) The person <u>who</u> answered the phone was Jim.

(2) Give this *to* <u>whoever</u> <u>*gets the first prize*</u>.

   (*Think*: <u>Who</u> *gets* the first prize?)

   (3) The teacher <u>whom</u> *you are referring to* has retired.

   (*Think*: You are referring *to* <u>whom</u>.)

(4) I would welcome <u>whomever</u> *you invite to the party*.

   (*Think*: You invite <u>whomever</u>.)

      (5) <u>Who</u> did you say *is on the phone?*

   (*Think*: <u>Who</u> is on the phone?)

      (6) <u>Whom</u> do you suppose *she was calling?*

   (*Think*: She was calling <u>whom</u>?)

      (7) She is someone <u>whom</u> *you would be meeting*.

   (*Think*: You would be meeting <u>whom</u>?)

Wise Up – This phrase means *to learn and change or be smart*.

Ex.   (1) Sylvia must <u>wise up</u> and junk her philandering lover.

Wish and the *Past Form of the Verb* – The verb *wish* (in the subjunctive mood) is used with the

   past tense of the verb describing the *action of the noun or pronoun that is the direct object* of

      wish.

Ex.   (1) I <u>wish</u> Ida <u>smiled</u> more often.

Wish and the *Future Form* of the *Verb* – *Wish* is used with *would* plus *the main verb*.

Ex.   (1) Her parents <u>wish</u> she <u>would pass</u> the test.

Wishful Thinking *Is Correct; Not* **Wistful Thinking** – *Wishful thinking* means *thinking based on*

desire but not on facts. Wistful connotes *desiring a little sadly what is not possible* or

frustrated desire.

Ex. (1) Make me run for Mayor, that's <u>wishful thinking</u>!

(2) The dejected man appeared <u>wistful</u>.

Within A Heartbeat – This expression suggests an *opportunity within one's grasp.*

Ex. (1) Completing his course was <u>within a heartbeat</u> so that he went the extra mile to make it.

With Regard To – *With regard to,* which means *referring to* or *concerning* must not be confused

with *with regards,* as the latter expresses *one's esteem or respect of another.* Expressions *with*

regard to, as regards, in regard to and *regarding* have the same meaning as *concerning,* but

not the same as *with regards.*

Ex. (1) <u>With regard to</u> the subject matter of inquiry, enclosed is our latest quotations.

(2) <u>As regards</u> the subject of inquiry…

(3) <u>In regard to</u> the subject of inquiry…

(4) <u>Regarding</u> or <u>concerning</u> the subject of inquiry…

With… Regards – *With regards* expresses *one's esteem of* or *goodwill* to another and must not

be interchanged or confused with *with regard;* the latter means *concerning,* a preposition.

Ex. (1) Send him this Christmas beer pack <u>with your regards</u>.

(2) This photograph is given to you <u>with my regards.</u>

<u>Write Down</u> – Write down means *to criticize* or *judge* a person in a disparaging way.

Ex. (1) Aleah Liz <u>wrote down</u> Mark Lester as a good-for-nothing playboy.

<u>Write Off</u> – *To record a cancellation of* a thing is *to write it off.*

Ex. (1) The manager approved the <u>writing off</u> of Fidel's debt.

- O -

☐ Table of Some Irregular Verbs. – Here are some irregular verbs *showing change in time* by **change in spelling** in *arbitrary* manner. :

• The suffix –ing is added to the base form of irregular verbs ending in consonant letters. In the case of the vowel-ended irregular verbs, the vowel ending is deleted before adding –ing. The ending consonant letter for the following irregular verbs is doubled before adding –**ing**: begin, cut, forget, get, hit, let, quit, run, set, sit, etc.

Past Participle	Present time		Past time
(base form)	(--s form)	(--ed form)	(used with helping verbs)
arise	arises	arose	arisen
awake	awakes	awaked, awoke	awaked, awoke
be (am)	is	was	been
bear	bears	bore	born, borne
beat	beats	beat	beaten
become	becomes	became	become
begin	begins	began	begun
bid (offer)	bids	bid	bid

bid (command)	bids	bade	bidden,** bid
blow	blows	blew	blown
break	breaks	broke	broken
breed	breeds	bred	bred
bring	brings	brought	brought
broadcast	broadcasts	Broadcast broadcasted	Broadcast broadcasted
burst	bursts	burst	burst
cast	casts	cast	cast
catch	catches	caught	caught
choose	chooses	chose	chosen
cleave	cleaves	Clove cleaved cleft	Cloven cleft
come	comes	came	come
cut	cuts	cut	cut
do	does	does	done
draw	draws	drew	drawn
drink	drinks	drank	drunk
drive	drives	drove	driven
eat	eats	ate	eaten
fall	falls	fell	fallen

fight	fights	fought	fought
flee	flees	fled	fled
fly	flies	flew	flown
forget	forgets	Forgot forgot	forgotten
forego	forgoes	forwent	forgone
forsake	forsakes	forsook	forsaken
foresee	foresees	foresaw	foreseen
Freeze	freezes	froze	frozen
Get	gets	got	gotten,** got
Give	gives	gave	Given
Go	goes	went	gone
Grow	grows	grew	grown
hang (a picture)	hangs	hung	hung
hang* (a criminal)	hangs	hanged	hanged
Hide	hides	hid	hid, hidden**
Kneel	kneels	kneeled, knelt**	kneeled, knelt**
Know	knows	knew	known
lay (to place or put)	lays	laid	laid

Lead	leads	led	led
Leave	leaves	left	left
Lend	lends	lent	lent
Let	lets	let	let
lie(recline)	lies	lay	lain
lie (false)	lies	lied	lied
lose	loses	lost	lost
prove	proves	proved	Proved proven***
quit	quits	quit	Quit quitted**
rid	rids	rid	Rid ridded
ride	rides	rode	Ridden**
ring	rings	rang	rung
rise	rises	rose	risen
run	runs	ran	run
say	says	said	said
see	sees	saw	seem
seek	seeks	sought	sought
send	sends	sent	sent
set	sets	Set	set
shake	shakes	Shook	shaken

shine (light)	shines	shone	shone
shine* (polish)	shines	shined	shined
show	shows	showed	shown showed
shrink	shrinks	shrank	shrunk
sing	sings	sang	sung
sink	sinks	sank	sunk
sit	Sits	sat	sat
spring	springs	sprang	sprung
stride	strides	strode	stridden
strike	strikes	struck	Struck stricken
strive	strives	strove	striven
swing	swings	swung	swung
take	takes	took	taken
teach	teaches	taught	taught
tear	tears	tore	torn
tell	tells	told	told
think	thinks	thought	thought
throw	throws	threw	thrown
understand	understands	understood	understood
wake	wakes	Waked woke	Waked, woken

wear	wears	Wore	worn
weave	weaves	Wove	woven
weep	weeps	Wept	wept
wind	winds	Wound	wound
wreak	wreaks	Wrought	wrought
wring	wrings	Wrung	wrung
write	writes	Wrote	Written**

☐ Forming the *–ed, –ing* and *–s* Forms of Regular Verbs

• For the *–s form of regular verbs*, the suffix **--s** is simply added to the following root or base verbs. However, the *–ed* and *–ing forms* of these regular verbs are done by doubling the ending consonant letter before adding the suffix **–ed** or **–ing**, as the case may be.

Abet, abhor, abut, acquit, adlib, admit, airdrop, allot, aver, bag, ban, bar, bat, bed, befog, beg, bestir, bet, blab, blip, blot, blub, blur, bob, bog, bootleg, brag, brim, bud, bug, bum bus, cabal, can, cap, carnap, cat, catnap, chap, char, chat, chip, chop, chug, clip, clam, clap, clod, clog, clot, club, commit, compel, con, concur, confer, control, cop, crab, cram, crap, crib, crop, cup, dab, dam, dap, defer, deter, dib, dim, din, dip, dispel, dishevel, dog, don, dot, drag, drip, drop, drub, drug, drum, dub, dun, embed, extol, flag, flap, flat, flip, flit, flog, flop, fog, fret, frog, gab, gad, grab, grin, grip, grit, gum, gun, gut, gyp, ham, hem, hog, hop, hug, hum, impel, incur, infer, inter, jab, jag, jam, jar, jet, jib, jig, job, jot, jut, kid, kidnap, knit, knot, lag, lam, lap, leg, lob, log, lop, lug, man, map, mar, mat, mob, mop, nap, net, nip, nod, pad, pan, pat, patrol, peg, pen, pep, pet, pin, pip, pit, plan, plat, plod, plop, plot, plug, pod, pop, pot, prod, prop, propel, pug, pun, pup, quip, quit, quiz, rag, ram, rap, rat, rebel, refer, repel, rev, rib, rig, rim, rip, rob, rot, rub, rut, sag, sap, scab, scan, scar, scat, scram, scrap, scrip, scrub, scum, sham, shim, shin, ship, shop, shun, sin, sip, skid, skim, skin, skip, slag, slam, slap, slat, slim, slip, slog, slop, slot, slug, slum, slur, snag, snap, snip, snub, sod, sop, span, spar, spit, spot, sprig, spud, spur, squat, stab, stag, star, stem, step, stir, stop, strap, strip, strop, strum, strut, stud, stun, submit, sup, swab, swap, tab, tag, tan, tap, tar, tat, thin, throb, thrum, thud, tin, tip, top, transfer, transmit, trap, trek, trim, trip, trot, tub, tug, tup

(British), twit, up, vat, vet, wad, wag, web, wed, wham, whet, whip, whop, whir, whiz, wrap, etc. (Exception: offer), order)

• For the *–ed* form, consonant-ended verbs in which the consonants are preceded by double vowels need only the addition of suffix **–ed**. The suffix **–ing** is added in the same manner for the *–ing form*.

Aid, ail, anneal, appeal, appear, applaud, ascertain, assail, attain, avail, avoid, bail, bait, bargain, beam, bewail, bleat, bloat, boat, boil, book, boot, braid, brief, broil, buoy, cashier, caterwaul, chain, chair, cheat, cheep, cheer, circuit, claim, clean, clear, cloud, coat, coil, coin, cook, complain, conquer, constrain, contain, cheer, creak, croak, croon, daub, defeat, deem, demean, derail, despair, detail, detain, diet, disdain, doom, drain, duel, endear, enjoin, enshroud, entail, entertain, entrain, entreat, explain, exploit, fail, fear, flail, float, flood, floor, flout, foil, fool, forfeit, foul, freak, fuel, gain, gleam, glean, gloat, goad, groan, greet, groom, grout, hail, haul, head, heal, heat, hook, hoot, impair, implead, jail, join, keel, knead, laud, leaf, leak, lean, leap, leer, load, loaf, look, loom, loot, mail, maintain, maul, moan, moon, moor, moot, nail, near, need, oil, overcoat, overcook, overhaul, overload, pain, pair, parboil, peal, peek, peel, peep, peer, pertain, plait, plead, pleat, pool, pour, pout, preen, prevail, proceed, quiet, raid, rail, rain, railroad, reap, rear, recoil, recruit, redeem, reek, reel, refrain, rein, remain, rendezvous, repair, repeal, repeat, restrain, retain, reveal, roar, root, roil, ruin, sail, school, scoop, scout, scream, screen, seal, sear, seed, seem, seep, sheaf, shear, sheer, sheet, shout, shriek, shroud, smear, sneak, spear, sneer, snoop, soak, soar, soil, sour, spear, spoil, spoof, spook, spoon, spoor, spout, sprain, sprout, squeak, squeal, stain, steam, steel, steep, steer, strain, streak, stream, stoop, succeed, suit, sweat, swoon, swoop, tail, team, teem, thread, toil, toot, tour, trail, train, tread, treat, troop, tweak, uncloak, unveil, uproot, veer, view, void, wail, wait, wean, wheel, zoom, etc. (Exception: *bivouac*, in which *k* is added before suffix *–ed*, thus, *bivouacked*.)

• The vowel--ended regular verbs (in which the consonant before it is preceded by another vowel) need only the addition of suffix **–s** for the *–s form* and suffix **–d** for the *–ed form*, however, for the *–ing form* the ending vowel letter is deleted before adding **--ing**. Here are some e-ended verbs: *abase, abate, abide, abjure, abuse, accuse, acquire, adhere, admire, adore, advise, appraise, apprise, aspire, atone, average, awake*, bake, bare, base, bide, bike, cane, care, case, cave, cite, combine, confine, cube, culture, cure, dare, date, daze, debase, debate, decide, decrease, defile, define, defile, delude, deride, devise, disguise, divide, enable, encase, equate, excuse, file, guide, imbibe, incite,* *indite, increase, include, inquire, intone, invade, invite, invoke, like, line, live, make, mate, mine, mire, name, opine, oppose, ostracize, pile, pine, pipe, plague, poke, queue*, quote, race, rape, rake, rave, release, , rile, rue*, rule, save, shake, shape, share, shave, side, sue, tide, time, use, utilize, validate, ventilate, voice, wane, wave, waive, wine, wipe, wire, yoke, zone,* etc.

Belie,* cue, decree, die*, free, hoe, knee, lie*, pee, queue, rescue, rue, sue, tee, tie*, toe, tree, vie*, etc. (Exception: *coo, moo, taboo, tattoo, woo*, etc. to which the suffixes **–es** and **–ed** are added; the suffix **–ing** is simply added to the verbs *be, hoe, pee, see, tee, toe*, etc., including *boo, coo, do, echo, go, moo, taboo, tattoo, woo*, etc., except *belie, die, lie, tie and vie.*

For the irregular verbs *belie, die, lie, tie, vie,* etc. **ie** is changed to **y** before adding **–ing** for the present participle, progressive tense and gerund forms. Thus, belying, dying, etc.

About the Author

Ernesto L. Lasafin

Ernesto L. Lasafin is a retired public High School teacher. A former military personnel who decided to become an educator, that's why under a certain law, he is also a veteran soldier.

Milton Keynes UK
Ingram Content Group UK Ltd.
UKHW030833181124
451360UK00002B/348